Future Financial Literacy

Navigating Cryptocurrency and Blockchain

Blake Reed

from various sources. Please consult a licensed professional before attempting any techniques outlined in this book.

By reading this document, the reader agrees that under no circumstances is the author responsible for any losses, direct or indirect, that are incurred as a result of the use of the information contained within this document, including, but not limited to, errors, omissions, or inaccuracies.

Table of Contents

Introduction:

What Is This Book About?

The age of crypto is taking the world by storm. Every time you open Twitter, a new cryptocurrency is trending. It's in the news every day, everywhere. Every second advertisement you see is for a crypto-asset trading platform. It feels so sudden. Just a short while ago, crypto trading was a fringe hobby for a few. Now it's *everywhere* and it feels like *everyone* is talking about it.

Much like the rapid rise of the internet in the 1990s and early 2000s, this is a defining moment in history and economics. Ignore it at your peril! Whatever you think about the rise of new financial technologies right now, they are here to stay. We will all need to adapt to it eventually, so it's best to get started on learning the ropes sooner rather than later.

It may seem confusing or intimidating at first, but remember that you are not alone, and this is not the first major revolution in global finance. Before credit cards became ubiquitous, most of us didn't understand or trust them. Before online transactions and banking apps became common, we felt just as wary of them. Even bigger than the implementation of new technologies in finance, recall (or imagine) the upheaval caused when the gold standard was abandoned in favor of our current foreign currency exchange system, or when the barter system was phased out in favour of currency.

However strange this may seem, history — and by extension, finance, and economics — is somewhat cyclical. Blockchain, cryptocurrency, and the metaverse are all brand new and uncharted territories, but only in the technological sense. Humans are constantly changing and reinventing the way our world works. This is not the first major revolution in finance, and it likely will not be the last. It is, however, the one that is happening right now.

In This Book...

By picking up this book, you are already taking the first steps to future financial literacy. But what does that actually mean? You are about to learn some fundamentals about the core parts that make up our upcoming financial reality. While the new world is impossible to predict, we do know a few things.

One: Cryptocurrency will be important, and the most important among the myriad of currencies springing up is likely Bitcoin. As such, this book will teach you mostly about Bitcoin, as well as a little bit about other currencies. It will also teach you a bit about novelty coins and spotting scams.

Two: Blockchain technology will be at the core of our new financial world and will probably power a lot more than just the financial sector. This book will explain how blockchain technology works, what that means for our finances, and how we can apply this technology elsewhere.

Three: The metaverse is rapidly becoming more important and comes with an array of possibilities. This book will take you on a mind-blowing tour of the metaverse (no, it's not just Mark Zuckerberg's thing) and give you a taste of what our lives and financial sectors might look like in the metaverse.

Four: There is certainly a lot of money to be made, but there is even more to be lost. This book will give some tips on how to stay safe, avoid getting ripped off, and hopefully get started on building your future wealth.

Five: As amazing as this new world is going to be, there are some major obstacles that need to be cleared first. Along with all the wonderful opportunities and vast potential you will learn about in reading this book, you will also receive a healthy dose of realism. You will learn how to spot when the endless possibilities of the future become a bit too good to be true, so you can put your money where it will be safe and profitable.

Now sit back, relax, and prepare to learn. This book will help you make sense of the most significant new financial technology. By the end of your journey, this brave new world of finance will be demystified. Get ready to become literate and confident in your understanding of future finance!

Do's and Don'ts Before Reading

DO get excited! A whole new world awaits and there are many fascinating technologies and ideas to explore and learn about.

DO get ready to question how we define value, how we decide what is "real" or not, and whether that distinction is as important as we tend to think it is. Is any value we assign to any item as concrete as it feels? Is the physical world that much more important than the digital world when the digital world is evolving so rapidly?

DO be skeptical of new technologies, as the new age of finance is still emerging and can be quite turbulent. Many people are taking advantage of uncertainty and lack of financial literacy to cheat amateur investors out of their money.

DON'T panic. You may feel like it is too late to learn, that you have missed your chance to invest, or that these technologies are too complicated to understand. You are still ahead of the curve, and understanding the fundamentals of Bitcoin, blockchain, and the metaverse is not as hard as it might seem.

DON'T allow your skepticism to override your excitement. There are certainly scams out there and ideas that are too good to be true, but some of the things that seem impossible are rapidly becoming a reality.

DON'T do anything rash. Investing in crypto-assets will be a core part of our future wealth, but diving in head-first without prioritising literacy and understanding is a fast way to get yourself into hot water, quickly.

Above all, keep your mind open and your wits about you. Some things may seem unfathomable but are becoming a reality. Other things may seem concrete, when in reality they may be pitfalls. In reading this book, you will gain the financial literacy necessary to make these distinctions, navigate the future, and even grow your digital and physical wealth.

Chapter 1:

The Future Is Here, Now

When we think about "the future," we might think of something at some point after the here and now. A couple of minutes from now, or a couple of centuries, or anything in between. When we think of big changes such as, a complete revolution in our global financial system, we might think of something that is just a few years away. However, the future financial system is already at our doorstep.

The seeds of change were sowed more than a decade ago with the invention of blockchain and the emergence of asset digitisation. Though we were not always aware of them, the seeds have been sitting in the soil, slowly germinating, and putting down roots. Now, the growth has become exponential, and it will not be long before it takes over. To avoid being left behind, it's time to learn about, and enter, the new financial world with confidence.

The Importance of Understanding

You may have heard the phrase "going paperless". Just a few years ago, companies and banks started announcing how they were going paperless, and within a given amount of time, there would be no more hardcopy forms to fill in, no more physical records, no more mail. Everything became digital.

Before that, people started "going cashless." It's safer and more convenient not to carry notes and coins, so why do it? Now people have thin bank cards and payment apps and devices. Tap your card, tap your phone, tap your smartwatch. Scan the QR code to pay. Cheques are near obsolete, and some businesses refuse cash transactions for safety reasons.

Can you imagine navigating daily finances without an app to check your account balance? Or buying your weekly shop without your trusty bank card? Maybe a decade ago, but certainly not today! This is the type of change that is coming with the age of cryptocurrency, blockchain, and the metaverse. In the near future, it will be just as normal to pay for your weekly shop with your crypto wallet as it is to use a credit card.

The applications for the technologies that make up the incoming financial era don't end in finance either. Blockchain, for example, is used for maintaining business records, managing supply chains, and is even being used by some governments to improve transparency. Cryptocurrency is used for investing, buying, and selling, but the same technology is being used to fund litigation and trade artwork. The metaverse, contrary to popular belief, is not just Meta (the new name for Facebook), but a term referring to a state of the world in which most of our interactions and assets are digital. If you've ever played an online multiplayer game, you've already had a taste of the metaverse!

It should now be clear that digital finance is not so much approaching our metaphorical doorstep, it's knocking pretty loudly. You don't want to be caught lost, unaware, and confused when it comes in and makes itself at home. Luckily, it is not too late! Although the speed at which financial technology is growing is blindingly fast, it is not quite ubiquitous yet. There is still time to learn, get ahead of the curve, and grow your wealth.

Ahead of the Curve

In 1976, Ronald Wayne owned 10% of Apple stock. He was one of the three founders of the now-famous tech company. Within a mere twelve days of working with Apple, Wayne became worried that the company was too unstable, and that he would end up with the company's debt when it failed. Unlike Steve Jobs and Steve Wozniak, who both had nothing to lose, Wayne did stand to lose his own assets if things went south.

So, he sold his share for just $800. Today, that same share would be worth roughly $300 billion (Bry, 2022).

If you look at the price of Bitcoin when it first started compared to its current price, you can imagine what Wayne must feel. You may feel a similar way about the changes in the financial world. What if you missed your window of opportunity?

The good news is you haven't missed it. Perhaps in comparing yourself to the first few people who bought their Bitcoin for practically pennies, you may have missed out. However, in the grand scheme of things, you are still ahead of the curve. In picking up this book and choosing to learn and grow now, before the true revolution begins, you are already ahead of most people. You will not be left behind.

Consequences

As you will see in the deeper explanations in this book, there are consequences to being left behind (or not!). Changes in the way we think about finances and the economy is not only a shift in the way we pay for things and make our money. Though you may have missed the first window to invest in the new economy, some predict that second-wave investors — i.e., people who are investing right now — still stand to gain just as much as first wave investors did.

Wealth Opportunities

This book is not going to give you investment advice. At its core, this book is meant to explain the basics of how digital finance works. You can think of this as an economics crash course, but for the very near future. That being said, it is impossible to look at phenomena like Non-Fungible Tokens (NFTs) and cryptocurrency without considering personal wealth. Economics and finance, futuristic or not, are linked to wealth. Just as those who understand our current financial system can use their knowledge to generate wealth — through trading stocks or foreign currency exchange, for example — those who understand future finances can do the same.

It is important to note that there are some things that are unique to investing in digital assets, but ultimately it is not so different from investing in physical high-risk assets. The main difference, for now, is the magnitude of volatility, and the prevalence of scams and doomed projects. This is where future financial literacy will come in. You need to be able to differentiate between a project that is doomed to fail and a project that is actually promising.

Always bear in mind cryptocurrency and future financial technologies are not a get-rich-quick scheme, as many commentators on social media want you to believe. They are also not inherently fraudulent. In fact, they have fraud prevention measures built into their normal function. These technologies might seem more prone to fraud than physical investments, but that is a result of bad actors taking advantage of newcomers who lack financial literacy, not a result of the systems themselves.

Blockchains, cryptocurrency, and metaverses form part of a whole new financial system. They do not stand in isolation, and they cannot make you money on their own. This book is not going to tell you how to get rich. However, with the knowledge and understanding of the new financial system, you may be able to do that for yourself.

Summary

Though all these new developments might seem sudden, they are the result of years of development, and they are likely to become mainstream a lot faster than you think. It is easy to become stuck in either thinking that there is plenty of time, or that it is way too late to get started. That is not the case. While the future is rapidly approaching, getting started now will still put you ahead of the curve both in terms of general literacy and in terms of wealth opportunities. When approaching digital wealth-building, remember that just as much as there is money to be made, there is money to be lost, and while no book can tell you exactly how to invest, this one will give you the knowledge about these new systems that you need to be able to work out investment strategies on your own.

Chapter 2:

Fundamentals of the New

Financial System

The new financial system is made up of certain key components that are important to understand. In this book, we are going to focus on three: Bitcoin (and, to a lesser extent, other cryptocurrencies), blockchain, and the metaverse. These three concepts form the backbone of the new financial system. As the previous chapter showed, the foundations for our new financial world have been in place for more than a decade. This chapter will give you a brief overview of the three concepts mentioned above and show you how they all fit together. Future chapters will look at them individually in much more depth, so if something doesn't make 100% sense yet, don't worry, keep reading!

Bitcoin

Bitcoin is a type of cryptocurrency. In fact, it was the first cryptocurrency ever created, and the first successful implementation of blockchain technology (more on blockchain later). To understand Bitcoin, we need to look at cryptocurrency in more general terms. A cryptocurrency is a form of virtual money that is not connected to any central bank. This is the core feature that separates cryptocurrency from standard currency. If we look at US dollars, for example, even when dollars are in no way physical, but purely managed through online transactions and electronic wallets like PayPal, the dollar is inherently and inextricably tied to the Federal Reserve System. Conventional currencies are centralised and connected to a (central) national bank or monetary authority. Cryptocurrency is the opposite of this. Rather than being maintained by a central authority, cryptocurrency is completely decentralised. Instead, it makes use of a blockchain to maintain and regulate it between peers.

A national monetary authority like the US Federal Reserve System exists to stabilise and regulate the use of currency. Their most important duties are to regulate banks and other payment systems, protect consumers from predatory financial practices, and oversee fiscal policies so that the economy remains stable. No authority other than a central bank can produce money or take it out of circulation. The central bank sets national interest rates. In short: the current financial system needs central authorities so that we can all agree on monetary policies, the value of money, and keep the value of a currency stable (Board of Governors of the Federal Reserve System, n.d.).

Zimbabwe is a great example of why centralised banks are important. Between 2007 and 2008, the Zimbabwean government started printing more money. When more money is printed to solve a problem, the value of the currency plummets in a phenomenon known as hyperinflation. Whilst the Zimbabwean situation is very nuanced, and the printing of money is not the only factor that led to hyperinflation, it does illustrate the importance of a sound central monetary authority in the current system (The Zimbabwean - Nation Online, 2021). It also presents the flip side: what if the central monetary authority was corrupt or incompetent? Suddenly, your currency is worth less than the paper it's printed on.

Bitcoin arose as a challenge to centralised banking authorities. Rather than having a single powerful government agency regulate monetary policies, peers regulate it. Every transaction, every new Bitcoin that is produced, is vetted, and recorded publicly. There is no need for any trusted third parties.

Furthermore, the lack of central authority means that Bitcoin is not tied to a single geographical location. Bitcoin pricing and transactions are not linked to international foreign exchange rates in the same way that conventional currency is. This is significant because foreign exchange has historically been difficult to successfully regulate without causing financial crises or national deficits. Internationally, we have gone through three different standards for regulating exchange rates to prevent global economic crises like the Great Depression, but no method has been perfect. We can demonstrate this with the Great Recession of 2008, of which aftershocks are still being felt. Failures of banking institutions in certain key economies like the US deeply affected the economic state of the rest of the world (Balaam & Dillman, 2016). Despite attempts to avoid single points of failure that can bring the international economy down, these things still happen. Removing the need for regulation by creating a currency that relies on peer-to-peer verification provides a decent solution to this issue.

Bitcoin also challenges the role of commercial banks. Currently, banks are needed to manage our finances and transactions, and it is virtually impossible to do anything related to personal assets and finances without the involvement of a bank. We entrust our money to a third party and hope they can be trusted. Theoretically, accredited banks can be trusted because they are answerable to central banks and government regulations. However, a failure to properly regulate, investigate complaints, or enforce government regulations can result in banking practices that actively harm consumers.

Following in the footsteps of Bitcoin, many other cryptocurrencies have been founded. Some of them are genuine challengers to Bitcoin, such as Ether, but many of them are little more than experimentation and gambling. Dogecoin is an infamous example of a cryptocurrency that began as a bit of a joke but rapidly rose in price (followed by an inevitable crash) after gaining press and social media attention. Some have referred to investing in cryptocurrency as a form of gambling or super-high-risk investment. However, established, and vetted cryptocurrencies like Bitcoin are more stable and can be used as a viable alternative to conventional money.

Chapter 3 will explore the rise of Bitcoin and its significance in far more detail, but for now, the key takeaway is that Bitcoin is a stable alternative currency that emerged as a challenge to centralised monetary authorities and third parties. In order to fully understand Bitcoin, however, we also need to understand the foundation upon which it is built: blockchain.

Blockchain

"The blockchain" has become a bit of a mystical term akin to "the cloud." What does it actually mean? As with "the cloud", blockchain is not a singular technology. There is no one, almighty blockchain, just as there is no one, almighty cloud. When we say something is stored in "the cloud," we're referring to any system that uses servers and an internet connection to store information, provide services, and run various software. Similarly, when we refer to "the blockchain," we are actually referring to an advanced cryptographic system that is used for a specific purpose. Bitcoin uses a blockchain. Ethereum uses a blockchain. But what is a blockchain?

At its core, blockchain technology is an advanced cryptographic system that requires a lot of mathematics and computer science to fully explain. However, we can create a sort of model. Think about molecular physics, for example. Molecules aren't really little spheres stuck together as you see in textbooks and diagrams but thinking about them using a model like that is really useful. So, for a brief crash course on blockchain, we'll use a model as well.

Think of an accounting ledger or bank statement that records every transaction that has happened in a given company. Now imagine that the ledger was open for anyone to see, and anyone could verify an entry on the ledger. Since anyone can double-check the ledger to verify its accuracy, and any new entry on the ledger requires strict verification that involves most people with access to the ledger agreeing that the new entry is correct, it is virtually impossible to forge entries on the ledger. Whenever someone tries to alter the ledger, everyone else needs to check that this is a legitimate alteration, and it will only be allowed if it is legitimate and correct. A history of alterations and who altered the ledger is also permanently recorded. This is, essentially, what a blockchain is.

In more detailed terms, a blockchain is a series (chain) of entries (blocks) on a ledger. Each of the blocks can be viewed and verified by anyone with access to that specific ledger. In order to add a new block to the ledger, the record must be verified by over half of its peers on the blockchain through a rigorous mathematical process. These ledgers can be public (i.e., anyone can view them) or access-controlled (i.e., you must be given special access to view them). Either way, anyone who has access to a ledger can verify it. Furthermore, copies of the ledger are given to everyone with access, making it a "distributed ledger." There is no main or master copy of the ledger, every copy of it is correct, up to date, and verifiable, so no single entity can control or manipulate it. A good system will even have ways to ensure that no single person or entity can own or control more than half of the total copies of the ledger, meaning that no single entity can make illegitimate entries or alterations.

Additionally, blockchain is versatile and has applications beyond the financial sector. Businesses are using blockchain for supply chain management, hospitals are using them for securely storing patient information, and governments are using them to keep records of citizenship. However, the most prevalent application of blockchain technology is in cryptocurrency.

As later chapters will show in more detail, blockchains are used to regulate and record transactions that use cryptocurrency. The blockchain eliminates the role of a central authority by rendering any transactions inherently transparent and legitimate. It is impossible to commit fraud on a blockchain that anyone can verify. Every new unit of currency that is created and every transaction involving that currency is recorded. Essentially, a blockchain is a "trustless" system because no third party is required. As long as the system itself is cryptographically sound, every transaction is inherently verifiable by anyone with access to the blockchain.

If this sounds a bit strange or complicated, don't panic. It is complicated, but Chapter 4 will break down this summary even further, providing you with a more detailed understanding of blockchain. For now, the most important thing to know about blockchain is that it forms the backbone of cryptocurrency, and no cryptocurrency can work without a secure blockchain. Therefore, the future financial world will depend on blockchain technologies.

Metaverse

"Metaverse" is a term that is relatively new. It launched into the public spotlight when Facebook entrepreneur, Mark Zuckerberg, announced the renaming of his company to Meta, along with his intentions to create a "metaverse." However, the metaverse associated with Zuckerberg's Meta is only a small part of what a metaverse is.

The term was coined in 1992 by cyberpunk author, Neal Stephenson, referring to a universe that is wholly created by computers and is divorced from the real world. Alternatively, a metaverse can be defined as any space that is fully digital or online. Although the term originated in fiction, the concept of a metaverse is not fictional. As early as the 1980s, online forums and chat rooms became the first generation of tiny metaverses (Clark, 2021).

A good example of a metaverse is a massively multiplayer online game, especially one with a comprehensive socio-economic system, such as the lesser-known *ArcheAge* by XL Games. In *ArcheAge*, you can form families, get married, become a political leader, buy, and build homes, farm, trade, commit crimes, join guilds, take up a craft, and more. All of these aspects of society are secondary to the main questline of the game, with the point of the game being to participate in this amazingly complex virtual society (Reahard, 2013). Newer games like *Eco* by Strange Loop Games have taken this even further, creating a multiplayer world in which players must create a complex civilization from nothing but an uninhabited natural world, complete with leaders, taxes, infrastructure, a legal system, and more, preferably without destroying the environment (Strange Loop Games, n.d.).

From the above examples, we see a clear picture: a complex, vibrant universe that is fully digital, in which real people spend time and live their lives. In the context of the new financial world, however, the metaverse is a bit more specific. Rather than being multiple self-contained universes, the metaverse (in this context) refers to the ongoing and increasing digitisation of the real world. Assets become virtual; our reality becomes augmented by technology. Everything is connected to the internet and each other.

The metaverse as an aspect of the real world, rather than a self-contained universe, is neither far away nor a new concept. Electronic assistants like Amazon's Alexa and Apple's Siri, smart home devices like Philips Hue lights, augmented reality (AR) goggles like Google Glass, and real-time image recognition software like LeafSnap are already enhancing our lives. The COVID-19 pandemic further sped up the move to increasing online presence, remote work, and digital social lives. Now many of us buy our necessities online, hang out with our friends on social media and private servers, and attend meetings via video conferencing. Jobs that we thought could not be done remotely are now partially or fully remote.

This trend is unlikely to slow down. In fact, it is more likely to speed up. Soon, many — if not most — of our finances and assets will be digital. This is why it is so important to understand the emerging financial system. When most assets and transactions become digital, you don't want to be stuck with only physical assets and no idea how to navigate the metaverse.

Chapter 7 will explain everything you need to know about the metaverse and how it relates to your future financial wellbeing. For now, understand that as the world digitises, so too the economy will digitise. Within such a digital economy, secure digital financial systems like Bitcoin and the blockchain will form the core of our daily transactions.

Summary

We don't know what exactly the future financial system will look like, but we know it will be built on foundations that were built over a decade ago. The three main elements that will support the new financial world are Bitcoin (and other cryptocurrencies to a lesser extent), blockchain, and the metaverse. These three will combine to create digital assets and fully online trading and wealth-building.

Chapter 3:

Bitcoin — Birth and Rise to Fame

By now you know what a cryptocurrency is. You also know that Bitcoin is a cryptocurrency - the first, the most stable, and the most popular. Now, we are going to delve into Bitcoin a bit more and look at the finer details. This chapter looks at how and why Bitcoin was created, why it became so popular, and why it is (and is likely to remain) the most reliable cryptocurrency. In understanding Bitcoin and its birth, we can understand why this new financial system arose in the first place.

Bitcoin Defined

Bitcoin was created by an anonymous person (or group, according to some speculations) using the pseudonym Satoshi Nakamoto. Nakamoto proposed a system in which no third party is needed to make sure that a transaction is valid and not fraudulent. Rather than use a trusted third party to verify transactions, the system itself should be fraud-proof by design. However, using conventional (fiat) currency needs at least one third party.

Fiat money refers to a country's legal currency. "Fiat" is a Latin word referring to "an authoritative order." In other words, fiat money requires some form of legal declaration (and therefore a third party) to give it transactional value. Fiat currency's value is not tied to a commodity like gold, the way that currency used to be valued before the world abandoned the gold standard (Hwang, 2021). Instead, the value is regulated by a country's central bank and economic performance. Once fiat money has been issued and its value determined, it requires constant regulation and the involvement of additional trusted parties to help with administrative things, like preventing fraud and making transactions. There is no way to trade using conventional currency without the involvement of at least one third party (the monetary authority which issues and regulates the currency), even if you use cash. Most people, however, don't use exclusively cash, so they need to use a bank to process things like transfers and card payments. When you pay for something online, even more third parties need to get involved. E-commerce websites need certificate authorities (like Comodo) and payment processing services (like PayFast) to make sure purchases are secure. Adding on to the already long list of third parties, banks will often have their own additional measures for online purchases, involving even more third parties (such as 3D Secure). If any of these parties can't be trusted, the validity of a transaction and the value of the money you use to make that transaction also can't be trusted.

So, considering that the current financial system requires at least a central bank as a third party (but usually more than just the central bank), any payment system that doesn't need third parties to be involved would require a whole new currency. Enter Bitcoin.

Bitcoin refers to both the currency and the system it runs on, which can be a bit confusing. This is one of the reasons why alternatives to Bitcoin tend to separate the system from the currency. Ethereum, for example, is the system that uses Ether as its currency. It can get difficult to keep track of whether someone is talking about Bitcoin as a system and Bitcoin as a currency but don't worry. This section will very clearly explain both and differentiate between them. Once you understand the difference, it is easy to know which one is being talked about in a given situation — it's about context.

The System

Before you can use and buy Bitcoins (the currency), you first need a Bitcoin wallet. The wallet is used to store your Bitcoin and perform transactions. It can be a program, app, website, or physical device of your choosing. Once you have your wallet, your first Bitcoin address will be generated. Your Bitcoin address is a public and unique identifier linked to your wallet. When you are involved in a transaction, this string of seemingly random characters will be recorded in the blockchain. You can think of the public address as a bit like a bank account number. For people to be able to pay you, you need to give them your banking details. They cannot use those details to access your money though.

At the same time, a private key will be generated. The private key is linked to your Bitcoin address but is not the same. This must be kept secret. It is similar to a password, CVV code, or ATM pin. If you want to spend any of your Bitcoins, you need to use your private key to verify that you own the Bitcoins you're trying to spend. This is referred to as "signing the transaction."

Public and private keys are foundational to any form of encryption and verification. You may not know it, but even simple day-to-day interactions use some form of this. For example, a messaging app on your phone that is end-to-end encrypted (most are), makes use of the same kind of thing to ensure that your messages cannot be intercepted or read by third parties. Your public address and private key work on the same principle, except much more complex and secure.

Once you have your wallet, you can use it to make transactions. A transaction refers to any transfer of Bitcoin between two Bitcoin addresses. All transactions are publicly broadcast and viewable on the blockchain. Bitcoin as a system is intrinsically linked to the blockchain that Bitcoin uses. For the sake of brevity, this chapter will refer to this as "the blockchain," but remember that there are actually multiple blockchain systems, and the Bitcoin blockchain is only one of them. It just takes too long to say "the Bitcoin blockchain" every time!

Whenever a transaction takes place using Bitcoin currency, or a new piece of Bitcoin currency is created, it has to be recorded and verified by the blockchain. We'll discuss what this means exactly when we talk about a blockchain verifying something in the next chapter. In broad terms, verifying a transaction is a five-step process that works like this:

1. A transaction between Bitcoin addresses takes place and the details of the transaction are broadcast to Bitcoin miners. Note: in this case, "miners" refers to the machines that perform calculations, not people who own and run mining setups.

2. Bitcoin miners create a new block on the blockchain which contains the transaction details.

3. To verify that the transaction is valid, all miners must perform intensive cryptographical calculations. This involves checking the public keys and making sure that the person paying actually has the Bitcoin they say they do. Other than that, more calculations need to be done as well, because the value of Bitcoin relies on processing power (more on mining later though).

4. Once a miner succeeds in solving the necessary calculation, the miner receives proof of work. Only the first miner to complete the calculations correctly will be rewarded.

5. The successful miner broadcasts its proof of work to other miners, who will check it. If over 50% of miners achieve the same result that the original miner did, the transaction is verified and can be added to the blockchain. If it isn't valid, the block won't be added.

Here is an example scenario that explains all the parts of any given transaction:

Alice is a merchant who sells jewellery and accepts payment via Bitcoin. Bob is about to use Bitcoin to purchase a necklace from Alice. Alice and Bob will agree to terms and then proceed with the transaction. For the sake of simplicity, let us say that the price of a necklace is set at 1 BTC. Alice's wallet value will increase by 1 BTC, while Bob's will decrease by 1 BTC.

Bob will use Alice's public address to send her 1 BTC. At the same time, Bob's wallet will sign the transaction using his private key, proving that he has 1 BTC and that the transaction is legitimate. Both of their public addresses, along with the value of the transaction (but not the private key), will be broadcast to the blockchain. Miners connected to the blockchain will then verify the transaction as described above. Once verified, Alice will receive 1 BTC and the transaction will be recorded. If the transaction somehow cannot be verified, it will not be recorded in the blockchain. It will be as though it never happened.

As you can see, Bitcoin relies on a network of miners to work effectively. Without miners, new blocks cannot be created. A transaction might get "stuck" and fail to complete for a while if miners don't verify them. As a way to incentivise mining, people receive an amount of Bitcoin currency as a reward. While this does mean that a lot of redundant work gets done, the value of Bitcoin is tied to processing power and energy, so it is necessary. There are some systems that are more efficient than Bitcoin, but those aren't really relevant right now.

The Currency

Bitcoin currency, officially abbreviated as BTC, refers to the money used in transactions on the Bitcoin network. Bitcoins are created and given to miners to reward them for their work. The amount of Bitcoin you can get from mining depends on how much you can mine and how quickly you can do it. The more you can mine, the more Bitcoin you can make. In other words, the value and scarcity of Bitcoin are directly tied to processing power.

That being said, there is a finite amount of Bitcoin. At some point in the future, the last Bitcoin will have been minded. There can only ever be a maximum of 21 million BTC in circulation. This may seem like a small number, but it actually isn't. With the way that the system works, the complexity of calculations that are required to obtain BTC compounds over time. In other words, it becomes more difficult and more time-consuming to obtain BTC from mining as more BTC is created, so the scarcity of BTC regulates itself and stabilize the value of BTC even when a lot of people are mining. Furthermore, the total possible reward for mining halves every four years (this is known as a halving event). Every four years, smaller and smaller units of BTC are received as rewards for mining. So, it becomes more difficult to mine, and you get fewer rewards for mining as time goes on. This trend of increasingly small fractions will continue until 21 million whole BTC has been mined. While the exact date is impossible to predict, experts estimate that the final BTC will be mined sometime around the year 2140, over a century from the time of writing (Wallabit Media LLC, 2022).

The great part is that, even when the last BTC has been extracted, people will still be able to buy and sell BTC amongst each other, in the same way that you can exchange other currencies. When we travel abroad and need to change our money from GBP Pounds to Euros, for example, we are actually buying Euros with our GBP Pounds. They don't need to print a new note or make you earn it every time you want to convert your currency! This same principle is how we can obtain BTC after mining is no longer possible, and how people can get BTC now if they don't mine.

The inner workings of this come down to some complicated mathematics and algorithms that you don't necessarily need to know to understand the way everything fits together. However, if you are interested, all the code and formulae are freely available for anyone on the official Bitcoin wiki.

Emergence and Rise of Bitcoin

In 2009, Satoshi Nakamoto published his famous whitepaper titled *Bitcoin: A Peer-to-Peer Electronic Cash System*, which detailed the reasoning behind the creation of Bitcoin, and its inner workings as a system and currency. When the first block of Bitcoin was mined by the inventor, a message was embedded in the block:

"The Times Jan/03/2009 Chancellor on brink of second bailout for banks."

This is a reference to an article published in The Times in 2009, which broke the news that British Chancellor of the Exchequer, Alistair Darling, was forced to bail out major banking institutions for the second time, costing £37 billion (Elliott, 2009). During the Great Recession caused by the 2008 Global Financial Crisis, governments were forced to pump money into commercial banks, because they were "too big to fail." In other words, the financial system relied so heavily on commercial banking that, if the industry were to go under, the whole economy would go down with it (Hardy, 2021).

Nakamoto was directly criticising the financial system which relied so heavily on commercial banking and created Bitcoin as an alternative to it. Bitcoin does not require reliance on any third parties, only a network of peers who use it. Therefore, users have direct control over their finances without needing to trust a bank.

Bitcoin was not a new idea when it launched, but it was the first practical implementation of cryptocurrency. As mentioned in the previous chapter, the concept of a blockchain dates back to 1982. The concept of computational puzzles being an expression of monetary value emerged in 1992 in a paper by Cynthia Dwork and Moni Naor. Nakamoto drew from these sources for his invention of Bitcoin, but it was ultimately a deep disappointment in the failures of the financial system that provided the spark to implement these theoretical ideas.

This is one of the reasons that a new financial system is imminent. Not only is the current system deeply flawed (evidenced by the required bailouts in the wake of the Global Financial Crisis), but the foundations of the future system we are preparing for were laid specifically to address the shortcomings of the current system.

In its first two years, Bitcoin was worth very little. However, in 2011, its value began to rise and fluctuate, wildly. This trend of unpredictable fluctuation in value continued for several years, though its value has continued to rise despite spikes and crashes. As its value reached astronomical highs, headlines about Bitcoin millionaires and billionaires began to pop up in mainstream media. So, more and more people took an interest in Bitcoin and cryptocurrency in general, and more alternatives to both Bitcoin and the current financial system began to emerge.

Now, additional services like The Lightning Network (which speeds up Bitcoin transactions) and Luno (which aids cryptocurrency trading) are emerging, improving the accessibility of Bitcoin and addressing some of the technical issues. El Salvador has declared Bitcoin acceptable legal tender. Banks have begun to deal in cryptocurrency as well as fiat currency. Bitcoin even set off a cascade of interest in blockchain research, leading to diverse academic fields and brand new ideas for the potential applications of this technology.

It is clear that the invention of Bitcoin and its rise to fame set off a chain of events that have irreversibly altered our economic system and will continue to do so. Soon, the compounding changes and developments will render our current system outdated and replace it with a new financial system. The question is, will Bitcoin keep its place as the so-called "King of Crypto?"

Here to Stay?

Bitcoin is currently the market leading alternative to fiat currency. It is often referred to as "digital gold" because of its high value and advantage compared to its competitors. While many argue that Bitcoin remains the best cryptocurrency despite the rise of serious competitors and subsequent fluctuations in Bitcoin's value, there are serious criticisms about its limitations.

Many, if not most, new cryptocurrencies are little more than novelties (or worse, scams). However, the main competitor to Bitcoin is Ethereum. Ethereum is technically the name of an entire ecosystem of programs that run on the Ethereum blockchain. The actual currency is known as Ether (abbreviated as ETH). In later chapters, Ethereum will be discussed in more detail, but at this point, it is important to note a few things.

Ethereum, while not yet as stable and prominent as Bitcoin, is similar in value but lacks some of the limitations of Bitcoin, such as the finite number of possible Bitcoins. Ether, by contrast, is unlimited. While the Bitcoin blockchain can only store Bitcoin transactions, the Ethereum blockchain can store pretty much anything. Ethereum even allows people to run their own programs on their blockchain, making it incredibly versatile and useful to entrepreneurs. By comparison, Bitcoin is not as flexible and diverse in its applications.

However, in terms of purely financial applications, Bitcoin remains superior and is likely to remain that way for quite some time. There are multiple reasons for this. Firstly, Bitcoin was created specifically as an alternative to the current financial system and is essentially a specialised machine. Ethereum, however, was not created with finance as its core goal. While Ether is a cryptocurrency of note, Ethereum's main purpose is to become a platform for people to create and manage digital assets.

Secondly, Bitcoin has a significant advantage. Because the crypto market is still volatile, new investors feel safer investing in big names that have proven themselves. People tend to be a bit more reluctant to invest in alternatives to Bitcoin. Ethereum is providing considerable incentives to invest in it, but ultimately Bitcoin's head start is a compounding advantage. It will be very difficult for any alternatives to truly catch up.

Lastly, it is very difficult to challenge a market leader. Alternative cryptocurrencies are cropping up all over the place, but the high investment risk and marketing advantage pose a significant barrier. This becomes especially problematic for potential challengers when there is so much publicity surrounding scam currencies, like the notorious SQUID debacle of 2020, in which a new currency (SQUID) built up a lot of interest in a short amount of time and had its price skyrocket overnight. At this point, the plug was pulled, and investors were left with tokens they spent astronomical amounts of cash on that are now worth exactly nothing. The scammers disappeared with all the money. SQUID was a highly publicized disaster, but it was not the first (and likely not the last) of its kind. This, combined with how volatile the value of cryptocurrencies can be (even stable ones like Bitcoin), incentivises investors to put their money in safer places. Bitcoin, despite its limitations, is considered a "safe bet" compared to newer currencies. As such, Bitcoin is unlikely to lose its advantage at any point in the foreseeable future.

Summary

While Bitcoin is not the only cryptocurrency out there, it is the most stable and is likely to remain that way for the foreseeable future. Its main competitor is Ether, which runs on the Ethereum blockchain. Bitcoin refers to both the currency and the blockchain it runs on. It emerged as a direct challenge to shortfalls in the current financial system, in the immediate aftermath of the Great Recession. Bitcoin kicked off the crypto-revolution and is leading the charge in changing the current financial system. It's unlikely that Bitcoin will lose its advantage over other cryptocurrencies for quite a while.

Chapter 4:

Blockchain — Definition

and Impact

Blockchain, contrary to popular belief, was not created for Bitcoin. It is actually much older than that. The first blockchain-like protocol was proposed by David Chaum in 1982 to create a tamper-proof way of keeping records between multiple parties that did not require the parties to trust either each other or an outside party. In 1991, Stuart Haber and W Scott Stornetta expanded Chaum's concept and described a system of timestamped blocks secured with cryptography. Satoshi Nakamoto used this system to create the blockchain as we know it today for Bitcoin.

This chapter will provide a more thorough explanation of blockchain technology and how it is relevant to the new financial system. Furthermore, this chapter will look at other applications of blockchains, both current and potential. In our exploration of blockchain, the chapter will also look at Ethereum. Ethereum is still relatively new and not as stable as Bitcoin, but its different implementation of blockchain in a more universal and comprehensive way does provide a lot of insight into the potential of blockchain and how it might link with the metaverse.

Blockchain Defined

In Chapter 2, we looked at blockchain as a broad technology that is integral to future financial models. In Chapter 3, we spoke about the role that blockchain plays in Bitcoin specifically. Now, we're going to look at defining blockchain in more detailed terms and explore its current and future significance to the new financial system.

Blockchain is a peer-to-peer system used to securely store information. Anyone with access to a given blockchain can view the information stored on it and verify its accuracy. There are open blockchains, such as Bitcoin and Ethereum, which are completely public. You also get closed blockchains that are only open to specific members of an organisation (the applications of this will be discussed in more detail later in this chapter). Adding blocks to a blockchain and verifying them requires a lot of computational power, as blockchain technology depends on advanced cryptographic puzzles both for security and for creating the value attached to cryptocurrency.

Blockchain is made up of three technologies: cryptographic keys, digital ledgers, and peer-to-peer networks. Let's look at these individually for a moment and see how blockchain puts them all together.

1. *Cryptographic keys.* We discussed the role of public and private keys in Bitcoin transactions in an earlier chapter, but this concept is integral to blockchain technology as a whole, not just finance. For anything to be recorded in a blockchain, its authenticity must be verified, and this is done by checking the public cryptographic keys and digitally signing entries with private keys.

2. *Digital ledgers.* A digital ledger is essentially a big spreadsheet that every peer in a network has access to. Whenever something is added to a blockchain, it is recorded in a digital ledger. You may have also heard the term "distributed ledger," which simply means that the information contained in any digital ledger (this could be any form of database, not limited to blockchain) is stored and accessible in a decentralised way. In other words, there are multiple copies of the ledger that are all accurate and up to date, and these copies are not stored in one central location.

3. *Peer-to-peer networks.* In computer science, there are two main ways to set up a network: client-server and peer-to-peer. Peer-to-peer refers to a network in which every computer or user

(known as a "node") is considered equal. The opposite of this would be a client-server network. The server node is superior to client nodes and supplies clients with information and resources. A good way to demonstrate the difference is through an example of downloading a file. When you download a file from a single source (like when you download an app for your iPhone from the App Store), a server sends the file to you, the client. However, another way to share files is with torrenting. When you torrent a file, your computer is receiving and piecing together data from lots of other computers on the network (peers), rather than a single server. For torrenting to work well, peers on the network should "seed" the files they torrent, meaning they allow peers to download the file from them as well, thus speeding up future torrents. Blockchain works on the same principle. Each node in the blockchain's network is equal, and there is no centrally controlled server. For a blockchain to work well, nodes on the network must use their computational power to verify transactions. This is known as mining. The more nodes that mine and verify, can speed up transaction processing.

Blockchain combines these three technologies into one. *Cryptographic keys* are required for *peers on a network* to verify transactions so that they can be recorded in a *digital ledger*.

In addition to these three technologies, blocks in a blockchain are securely encrypted to ensure they cannot be tampered with. Furthermore, each peer on the network has access to a copy of the digital ledger, and thus, should a block be successfully altered, the change will be compared to the ledger copies owned by other peers. If more than half of the peers can confirm that the block was altered correctly and legitimately, the change is saved. If not, it will be discarded. Blockchains prevent illegitimate changes from succeeding by ensuring that no single person or entity can own more than half of the nodes on the network.

Blockchains work on the principle of consensus, so if a single entity was able to somehow control a majority of nodes, that would allow them to make illegitimate entries on the ledger or illegitimately alter entries. This is one of the many ways in which blockchain can be likened to a democratic system. If one person or group's vote in an election counted for more than other people or groups' votes, the outcome of the election would be unfair, undemocratic, and illegitimate. By ensuring that all nodes have equal say and no single entity can manipulate more than half of all nodes, blockchains ensure a perfectly trustless, decentralised, unalterable, and accurate means of keeping financial records and processing transactions.

Significance

Blockchain is a versatile technology, but its main significance lies in trustlessness and decentralisation. The current financial system requires us to trust at least one third party with our finances — more if we use electronic payment systems — and must give up control over our own resources. Furthermore, the minting of actual currency and its regulation and value has a single point of failure — the central bank. By decentralising control over currency regulation and production, there is no single target that can be attacked to derail a country's financial market.

Trustless

Currently, if I want to make a payment using my ordinary bank account, the following process takes place:

1. The bank receives a notification that I want to pay someone £5.

2. The bank checks to see if I have £5.

3. If I have £5, that amount is subtracted from my account and added to the account of the person I am paying. This can take several days if the recipient does not use the same bank that I do.

In this process, neither I nor the person I am paying has complete control. We must trust that the bank will process this payment correctly and in a timely fashion. We must trust that the records will be kept correctly. We must trust that the banks are not handling our money recklessly. The exact policies and safety precautions the bank takes to keep our information safe are kept secret to prevent attacks on their central systems.

If a bank cannot be trusted, such as in cases of predatory banking, or when banks use the money stored with them to participate in dangerous investment practices, our money is not safe. However, when a blockchain is used, the users are in complete control. There is no need for a trustworthy third party, there can be no forgeries, and anyone can check the code and cryptography to ensure that there are no flaws. Nothing can happen to the information stored on a blockchain without the incident being recorded. It is an automated, highly fraud-resistant, and totally transparent system.

In addition to this built-in transparency, blockchain is extremely secure, making use of state-of-the-art cryptographic algorithms to secure sensitive data, regulate value, and verify transactions. Proper encryption is vital to secure finance, even in traditional systems. It is cryptography that protects our account details and prevents online transactions from being intercepted. Furthermore, cryptography and calculations are at the very heart of cryptocurrency and blockchain technology, so it makes sense for the algorithms used to build blockchains to be of high quality and practically impossible to crack without the right keys.

Now, you may be thinking that blockchain cannot be truly trustless. You still need to trust the system itself and trust that its encryption is as good as it claims to be. It is good to have this sort of skepticism in mind when dealing with new technologies, especially considering how people have been taking advantage of all the excitement to rip off newcomers. However, this is the beauty of blockchains. Anyone with access to the blockchain can check that it is cryptographically sound. Even if you personally do not have the knowledge to check it, many of the people invested in blockchain technologies are cryptography enthusiasts, and therefore can and do investigate the blockchains they use, ensuring the soundness and security of the system.

Keeping the blockchain secure is not the responsibility of a single actor, and therefore has advantages in terms of safety nets (multiple copies of the blockchain being checked for authenticity at all times) and collaboration (multiple interested parties ensuring that it is solidly built and well-maintained). This is tied to blockchain technology's other most significant feature: decentralisation.

Decentralised

When something is decentralised, it means that there is no single point of failure. There is no "Bitcoin Headquarters" that can be attacked or "Ethereum

Server" that can go down. As long as there are peers on the network, there will always be a functional blockchain. This links up with trustlessness, in the sense that you do not need to place your trust in a central authority that controls everything.

Decentralisation addresses two issues with the current financial system. Firstly, it does not require a central authority to regulate financial policy and economics, such as a reserve bank. Secondly, it does not require a commercial bank to safely handle your finances for you. In both of these cases, if something goes wrong, the whole system goes down.

In the case of the reserve bank, recall earlier when we used the example of the Zimbabwean money-printing disaster. The Zimbabwean reserve bank played a central role in bringing down the country's economy, and while it was not the only factor contributing to the rapid decline of the Zimbabwean economy, a decentralised way of managing the production of value could have prevented the sudden and sharp devaluation of the Zimbabwean dollar.

In the case of commercial banks, there are multiple issues. Commercial banks, firstly, are so integral to our current financial system that they are considered "too big to fail." This means that, should the banking sector experience a major crash, governments will have no choice but to bail banks out, with ordinary citizens bearing the brunt of the consequences. Secondly, banks must use the money that we entrust to them in an accountable way and ensure that the money is safe, reliably invested, and responsibly loaned. When banks engage in unsafe practices, such as loaning more money than people can conceivably repay (a key factor leading to the 2008 financial crisis), our money is not safe with them. Lastly, transactions can fail due to issues on the bank's side, without any faults on the side of the people involved in the actual transaction. This can sometimes even result in unwanted charges, including administrative fees to rectify mistakes made by the bank itself.

In this discussion, we can clearly see why Satoshi Nakamoto created Bitcoin as a response to the failure of the current financial system, and how the future financial system is intentionally designed to address the failures of the current system. Both decentralisation and trustlessness, the most significant features of blockchain technology, are designed to compensate for the problems that led to the 2008 financial crisis.

Pioneer

Though blockchain technology was not invented specifically for the new financial system, its first and most successful application was its use in Bitcoin. As such, blockchain's overall significance to society is tied to its success as an alternative to the current financial system. Not only is it significant in its features addressing issues with the current system as discussed above, but it is also significant in forming the backbone of the new financial system. Furthermore, its pioneering success in finance has sparked research interest, opening the way for even more potential applications of the technology that can address flaws in systems other than the global financial system.

Ethereum

It is useful to also study Ethereum when we look at blockchains. Though Bitcoin is likely to remain the most dominant cryptocurrency for the foreseeable future, Ethereum is proving to be a strong competitor. Not so much because of its currency, Ether, but because of the versatility of its blockchain.

Ethereum was launched in 2015, following a 2013 whitepaper by founder Vitalik Buterin. In the whitepaper, Buterin acknowledges the radical contributions made by Bitcoin and explains his vision to use a similar methodology as a sort of operating system for the internet. Ethereum implemented the concept of "smart contracts" and "decentralised apps" (dapps). The Ethereum blockchain is more than a financial system like Bitcoin. While that is included and incentivises people to use it, that is not its main strength.

Programmable Blockchain

The Ethereum blockchain has its own programming language, which people can use to execute programs automatically. This is known as a "smart contract." Smart contracts are essentially bits of code stored in blocks on the blockchain that execute under certain conditions. Smart contracts can be combined to create dapps. Because there is no singular server on which the smart contracts are stored, data and applications cannot be removed or censored.

Ethereum is also used to create Decentralised Autonomous Organizations (DAOs). A DAO is an organization that has transparency and democratic decision-making built into its foundations. By codifying the rules and purpose of the organisation in a smart contract that can only be altered through a majority vote, and having resources managed in a decentralised way, no singular member can have more control than another. This opens up possibilities for global organisation and cooperation. When creating traditional organisations, there is a fair amount of trust and coordination involved. Resources cannot be embezzled, and decisions cannot be made unilaterally, especially without other members having full knowledge of what is happening. A DAO removes the need to trust the hierarchical structure by being transparent and democratic, thus encouraging membership.

Essentially, the driving purpose behind Ethereum's programmable blockchain is to create equal communities and programs that are as close to being immune to censorship as is realistically possible. Furthermore, with the addition of financial services (through Ether and through finance dapps and DAOs), Ethereum hopes to make finance more inclusive without requiring as much invasion of privacy as conventional finance does. People cannot be denied access to bank accounts based on proof of residence, education, employment, income class, or any other factor that can be used as a basis for discrimination. Accounts cannot be blocked or frozen, and as such people cannot be excluded the way they can in the current system. Anyone with internet access can be included in blockchain-based financial systems.

Significance

Ethereum demonstrates the diverse applications of blockchain technology, both in terms of how we can use it, and how it can improve diversity and equality. By decentralising power in an organisation and making censorship practically impossible, Ethereum is opening up the possibilities of what future society could look like. These possibilities will become increasingly important as we explore the metaverse in Chapter 7.

In terms of finance specifically, Ethereum is significant as the most successful alternative to Bitcoin so far. Diversity in finance — especially experimental investments such as through cryptocurrency — is important. It is not enough for a platform to simply be very good and diverse on its own. Prospective users must also be given meaningful choices. Otherwise, it's simply removing control from consumers yet again.

Prospects and Potential

Up until now, we have only briefly mentioned the potential applications of blockchain technology beyond the finance and digital asset sector, but remember that a block can represent almost anything, not just a transaction or expression of value, like a cryptocurrency. Our discussion of Ethereum broadened our understanding of how blockchain can be expanded to do more, but ultimately Ethereum is still strongly tied to the financial sector. This section will show other applications for blockchain technology, demonstrating that it is not just that the financial sector is changing, but that blockchain as a technology is so important to our future that it is making foundational changes to multiple industries, including governments.

Blockchain in Business

Blockchain has applications in virtually every industry. Retail and healthcare will likely benefit the most from blockchain-based applications, simply because of the sheer number of potential applications, but they will not be the only ones. Below are some brief examples of how blockchain is and can be implemented outside of cryptocurrency.

The ability of a blockchain to store unalterable records makes it ideal for tracking systems and databases. In travel and tourism industries, this can be used for tracing baggage across borders and identifying passengers to improve search-and-rescue operations. It can also be used for tracking shipments and managing supply chains. Security and cybersecurity companies can also use this for keeping entry and exit logs, storing data securely, and preventing the illegitimate alteration of data. The medical and pharmaceutical industries make use of this feature to keep secure, immutable records of patient history, manage drug supply chains to combat fraud and counterfeit medication, and maintain data integrity in research environments. Human Resources departments can also use this to store long-term employee records, preventing resume fraud. Conventional banks have also begun to employ blockchain technology to store transaction data and clients' account information securely and unalterably.

Blockchains' capacity for automation through smart contracts and programmable blocks makes them ideal for secure automated systems. This makes it ideal for any form of secure payment system, whether that be in the form of e-commerce, paying employees, cross-border payment systems, or maintaining tax profiles. Payment systems could also integrate with cryptocurrency. The ability to create dapps also allows for the creation of automated procurement systems, which might integrate with tracking and payment systems. In medical systems, this attribute can also be used to analyse and draw conclusions from patient records, allowing medical professionals to improve the accuracy of their research and diagnoses, even across borders.

Blockchain can also be used for verification purposes. This is great for digital rights management (DRM), piracy and fraud prevention, proof of ownership issuance, and identity management. Any user or record can be easily verified, thus allowing more secure transactions and immutable proof when something has been purchased (as opposed to illegally acquired), with no capacity for fraud.

Blockchain is not necessarily the current best or most efficient system in each of these cases, but this goes to show how many use-cases there are for secure, transparent, and unalterable record-keeping. We can expect to see more and more possible implementations popping up as people tailor blockchain technology to more specific needs and niches.

Blockchain in Government and Democracy

Blockchain is gaining increasing attention for its potential to improve the quality of democracy when implemented by a government. It is not just that blockchain can improve the efficiency of a government's duties to its citizens, but that an efficient and transparent government is inherently more democratic than one that is unable to respond to its citizens' requirements as effectively.

Blockchain's use-cases in government fall into two categories: improving government duties and improving citizen engagement. These two feed into one another to create more democratic and robust governments.

In terms of government duties, blockchain can be used to manage citizen identities and their associated rights and freedoms. For example, only citizens over a certain age are allowed to vote, only citizens with a valid drivers' license are allowed to drive a car. This can even be automated so that systems can update as licenses and identity information change or expire. Essentially, the need for multiple separate systems is replaced with one robust system. Blockchain can also be used to maintain land titles and other relevant proof of ownership. This can even be integrated into identity management systems, minimizing the risk of fraud and tax evasion.

The inherent transparency of blockchain can also be used to improve public procurement systems, again minimizing the capacity for corruption in government. This is especially useful in situations where governments have a history of corrupt procurement systems. Furthermore, blockchain can be used to store transparent records of government dealings and treaties, ensuring that state officials are automatically more accountable to citizens.

Blockchain is also being used to crowdfund litigation, allowing more people to get access to justice systems without being limited by their financial status. This means that corporations and the state cannot "win by default" if a citizen or smaller business runs out of money to continue legal proceedings. This is done by allowing people to "bet" on legal proceedings using crypto tokens, receiving a payout if they win the bet. This is a good way to improve the fairness of the justice system and help your fellow citizens while also making some extra cash.

Summary

Blockchain is an incredibly versatile technology with applications well beyond the financial sector. Its most important features lie in its security, immutable record-keeping, decentralisation, and transparency. Blockchain technology forms the backbone of crypto-assets, and we can expect to see more developments in how it is used, from finance and business to healthcare and government. The more that we experiment with ways in which blockchain can be used, the more robust and versatile blockchain systems become.

Chapter 5:

Wealth Building in the New Financial System

The point of a financial system is not only to trade goods and services to keep our daily lives running. It is also there for us to build our personal wealth. This extends to the new financial system as well, and you can begin to build wealth in the new system alongside any wealth you may have accumulated in the traditional system. This can be done by adding digital assets to your physical and monetary assets.

This chapter is not going to tell you how to invest in digital assets like cryptocurrency, or even which assets to invest in (beyond telling you how to figure out what to absolutely not invest in). The new financial system is still so new, and it is important to stay on top of the most recent developments in order to invest safely. Rather, this chapter will give a basic rundown of how wealth-building in the new system is likely to work, giving you a head start for when digital assets become the norm.

Digital Assets

There is more to investing in the new financial system than simply acquiring cryptocurrency, though that is a pretty big component of it. There are other types of assets that we can invest in as well in the new system. Let's look at what we mean when we talk about crypto assets. Then we can start looking at how we can invest in them, as well as some crucial do's and don'ts.

Physical assets can be sorted into asset classes. There are several ways to do this, and different systems will classify assets in different ways. However, the main point of classifying assets is to sort them according to characteristics, how they behave, and which regulations they are governed by. Gold, for example, is classified as a commodity, while shares in a company are classified as equities.

Asset classes can be divided into subclasses, which are even more variable and difficult to define than their parent classes. As an example, let's look at commodities as an asset class. Commodities can be divided into soft commodities, referring to agricultural products, and hard commodities, which are mined or extracted. Even hard commodities can be divided. Crude oil is a hard commodity in which the value is derived from the products that can be made with it — crude oil on its own isn't too valuable, but petrol is. Gold is also a hard commodity, but its value is inherent — gold is valuable regardless of what you do with it.

So which asset class do crypto assets belong to? Well, that's actually a pretty tough question. If we use Bitcoin as an example, Bitcoin's value is both in the currency and the blockchain software used to create and trade with it. The software could be compared to a commodity like oil, as its value is directly tied to what it is used for. The currency could be a cash equivalent, a commodity with inherent value (one of the reasons Bitcoin is referred to as "digital gold"), or even foreign exchange. However, we cannot separate the currency from its software. There is no cryptocurrency without its blockchain. As such, crypto assets are grouped into their own, brand-new class: digital assets.

We're going to discuss the digitisation of assets in much more depth in Chapter 7, but for the purposes of wealth-building in the new financial system, we do need to know some basics. Digital assets are intangible. You could use an asset like cryptocurrency to buy tangible assets, but cryptocurrency is not the only digital asset out there. Non-Fungible Tokens (NFTs) are a form of digital asset as well, though they are more comparable to art trade and property investment.

The most common form of investment in digital assets is through cryptocurrency. There are two main ways to do this: through trading, and through retaining. When you trade cryptocurrency, it's quite similar to trading stocks or foreign currency. You buy a certain amount of cryptocurrency when the price is relatively low, and sell when it is more expensive, turning a profit. Retaining cryptocurrency is similar to buying gold. You could sell it, but you could also keep it and allow it to appreciate in value over time. Alternatively, you can mine it yourself and sell or retain it, but that's pretty difficult to do in a profitable and sustainable way.

Currently, trading cryptocurrency is a very popular form of investment. The last couple of years saw a boom in people interested in trading cryptocurrency, especially Bitcoin and the novelty currency, Dogecoin. However, when the concept was still very new, people would buy a couple of units of Bitcoin at a low price and just allow it to appreciate in value over time. You may have heard stories of crypto-millionaires — people who made a lot of money either trading digital assets or people who bought some novelty coins and allowed them to appreciate over several years, and only cashing out when the value rose to dizzying heights more than a decade later.

Buyer Beware

What is important to note about cryptocurrency trading is that it is incredibly volatile, even when compared to similarly high-risk investment strategies, such as trading stocks. This goes double for newer currencies, as they are much less stable than more established currencies like Bitcoin. As such, prices are liable to high spikes and very low crashes; there is a danger of losing your money if you aren't careful.

Besides the volatile market, there are also some other dangers to investing in cryptocurrency. Firstly, crowd speculation. This occurs when a large number of amateur investors start putting a lot of their money into speculative investments. As a result, the price goes up substantially. If the price starts to fall, or more experienced speculators decide to sell their assets, a sort of crowd panic begins to spread, causing prices to drop and more people to sell. Usually, inexperienced investors end up losing a lot of money in situations like this. In fact, this is one of the factors that led to the Wall Street Crash of 1929.

Secondly, gambling mentality. While it is true that high-risk investment is always a bit of a gamble, the mistake that many gamblers make is not cutting their losses or quitting while they're ahead. Unfortunately, many crypto enthusiasts have a tendency not to learn from previous crashes or that completely different rules apply to the crypto market compared to traditional investment. While some aspects are very different, ultimately human economic behavior has been well studied and remains predictable across markets. It may be difficult to assign value to digital assets the same way that we do to traditional assets, seeing as it is a completely new asset class, but people are still people, and people tend to react predictably to volatile markets.

There is certainly money to be made in crypto assets, but there is also much to be lost in such a high-risk market. To avoid losing too much money, you must keep a level head. You must understand the dangers and react to the inevitable fluctuations calmly and rationally, just as you would with traditional assets.

Investing in Cryptocurrency

Despite crypto assets being so new to our financial system and relatively unstable compared to traditional assets, many of the usual investment rules of thumb still apply. Firstly, don't put all your eggs in one basket. Secondly, ensure that your investment is robust. Thirdly, keep it safe. Lastly, understand the asset itself.

Egg Baskets

When referring to investments, when people say, "don't put all your eggs in one basket," they don't just mean not to put all your money in one single asset. They're also talking about asset correlation. You want to avoid any situation with a positive correlation. Rather, your assets should have either negative or zero correlation.

Correlation refers to how assets respond to market conditions. The values of different asset classes will behave differently under different circumstances. In some cases, asset classes might react in directly opposite ways. When there are no similarities in the ways assets react to changes in economic circumstances, those assets have no correlation. When assets behave in opposite ways, they have a negative correlation. When your assets all react the same way, that is called a positive correlation.

A diverse portfolio will avoid positive correlation as much as possible. You really don't want a situation where changes in the international economy cause the value of all your assets to plummet. You'll lose a lot of money if that happens. Instead, you want to be in a situation where, even if one asset loses its value, other assets will be unaffected, or even increase in value.

A good way to diversify your portfolio is to either add digital assets to your traditional investments if you have some or to add traditional assets to your digital assets. There is zero correlation between crypto-assets and traditional markets, so even if something goes wrong with your traditional portfolio, you'll be okay. There have also been some instances of negative correlation, where frustration with traditional markets has led to more interest in crypto-markets, increasing the value of crypto-assets. Inversely, if you are burned by the volatility of crypto markets, you will not have lost any of your traditional assets.

Robustness

Crypto assets, while relatively easy to acquire nowadays, can be a bit tricky. To obtain cryptocurrency, you can either mine it yourself (which requires a specialised and dedicated mining rig) or purchase it with fiat currency. Other crypto-assets, such as more niche and lesser-known currencies or NFTs might not be purchasable with fiat currency, requiring you to use common cryptocurrencies like Bitcoin or Ether to purchase them in the first place.

The reason it can be difficult to acquire niche cryptocurrencies is that many exchanges avoid making currencies available until their value has stabilized. Because of this, a good way to check if the currency you are about to purchase is reliable is to check how many fiat or cryptocurrencies can be used to purchase it. This is known as checking *trade pair diversity*. The more fiat and cryptocurrencies can be used to buy a given asset (i.e., the more trade pairs it has), the more robust that currency is likely to be. A robust currency is a safer investment, as it is less likely to fail or cost you a lot of money.

Safekeeping

Crypto assets must be stored in a crypto wallet. There are many wallet applications, websites, and physical devices available to use. Some may have more utility than others, allowing you to trade from within the wallet or store multiple assets in the same wallet, as opposed to having separate wallets. However, the most important thing a crypto wallet should have is not utility, but security.

Remember that, while blockchains are very secure, your assets are linked to you through your wallet. So, while it is practically impossible to illegitimately alter a blockchain and steal money in that way, the same does not apply to your wallet. If money is transferred from your wallet, that money is gone. It cannot be retrieved or reversed. If this was done illegitimately, you likely will not be able to identify the thief or get the money paid back. As such, you must have a secure wallet.

A good wallet will not require excessive personal information, and the developers will be transparent about which security protocols are in place to protect your information and keep your assets safe. You should also steer clear of any wallets that have experienced successful attacks or data breaches, or wallets made by disreputable developers. Ensure you read up on the wallets you are considering and that there have been no major complaints.

Beyond ensuring that the wallet you choose is secure, you must also choose between a "hot" wallet and a "cold" wallet. A hot wallet is connected to the internet, meaning it is much easier to access your assets anywhere, anytime. However, having access to the internet leaves a wallet vulnerable to attacks by hackers. A cold wallet, by contrast, is not connected to the internet at all. This makes your wallet inaccessible to hackers unless the physical device it is on is stolen and accessed. While this is good security-wise, it makes it more difficult to access your assets.

Usually, it is best to opt for a combination of the two. Having some of your assets inaccessible to anyone but you and some of them readily available protects you from attacks while also allowing yourself freedom and ease of use. Note that many crypto-exchange platforms have built-in wallets that use combined storage methods. Ensure that the platform you use does not store too much in hot wallets, as they are more likely to be targeted by cybercriminals.

When setting up your wallet and the device on which you store your wallet, ensure you take your own security measures. Use a unique password that you have not used elsewhere and is difficult to guess. Good passwords should not contain common dictionary words, dates, or names. The most difficult passwords to crack are long passwords. A 6-character password that has a combination of uppercase letters, lowercase letters, numbers, and special characters is much easier to hack with brute force techniques than a less complex 20-character password.

Understanding the Asset

There is a lot to know about any given crypto asset, and it is important to know what you will be getting into when you buy it. This step of the investment process is truly crucial because this is how you avoid scams and short-lived, poorly executed projects. In other words: the difference between making money and losing it.

Firstly, you must read the associated whitepaper. When a new crypto project is founded, the developers will release a whitepaper explaining how it works and what the goals are. The Bitcoin whitepaper, for example, contains an explanation of why Bitcoin is necessary, what it seeks to achieve, and an explanation of the cryptography behind it. The Ethereum whitepaper does the same. Any legitimate project will have a whitepaper that is easy to find, well-formatted, free of mistakes, easy to understand, and precise. A whitepaper that is filled with errors and vague language or is too confusing to understand should be an immediate red flag, as it shows a lack of effort and planning on the part of the developers.

Secondly, you want to check whether the asset has a "decentralisation edge." In other words, it must have some level of usefulness as a service and must be set apart from other assets in a meaningful way. Looking at Bitcoin again, it has a clear purpose as a challenge to the centralised nature of the current financial system. Ethereum, while its currency Ether is a good competitor for Bitcoin, sets itself apart by having a different purpose and some other relevant services. If an asset seems like it isn't really useful or doesn't have any sort of advantage over similar assets, there is likely a better asset you could invest in. Remember that the value of a digital asset is strongly linked to perceived importance, so if public opinion deems a digital asset to be unnecessary or not useful, its value will decline.

Next, ensure the developers and the community are actively engaging with one another. A promising asset should have competent developers who have open channels of communication with the community. The community should actively contribute to the asset by mining, providing information, and suggesting improvements. Developers should be open to feedback and display a thorough understanding of the fundamentals of cryptocurrency.

Lastly, the currency should have a fair issuance model. The issuance model refers to the way in which currency is distributed and how much of it can exist. For example, there can only ever be 21 million Bitcoins, compared to unlimited Ether. A fair issuance model should not disproportionately reward miners and developers, as this can result in a concentration of currency and power that jeopardizes the trustless nature of a blockchain. Furthermore, there should not be too much initial supply. If the initial supply is too high, the market will be oversaturated, and the value of the asset will likely not appreciate.

With these tips in mind, let's have a look at an infamous case study. In 2021, following the landslide success of the South Korean Netflix series *Squid Game*, a novelty cryptocurrency known as SQUID emerged. The SQUID developers used pop-culture imagery to gain media attention and, by extension, the attention of investors. Within the space of a week, the price of SQUID rose by 2000%. On the evening of the 31st of October, the price spiked by 310000% and then immediately fell to being worth exactly nothing after the developers disappeared with the $3.38 million investors poured into it (Aratani, 2021; Valinsky, 2021).

Hindsight is always 20/20, but in this case study, experts were calling SQUID an obvious scam right from the start. Let's apply our knowledge and have a look at the signs.

1. The SQUID whitepaper was vague, poorly formatted, and filled with errors.

2. SQUID tokens could be bought, but not sold. Instead, buyers would have needed to earn the ability to cash out by playing online games inspired by *Squid Game*.

3. SQUID was not purchasable on reputable crypto-trading platforms. Some platforms issued warnings to users to exercise caution if they were intending to buy SQUID.

4. Developers did not allow the community to interact with them. Though they had a Telegram group and a Twitter account, neither of these allowed any comment or engagement.

5. The price of SQUID rose rapidly and unsustainably. We know that the value of any given cryptocurrency tends to be quite volatile, and that sudden uncontrolled growth is always followed by a crash.

6. The whole project capitalised on a hot topic in news and pop culture, making use of the existing media attention and flashy publicity stunts to draw attention to itself. Mainstream news coverage tended to focus on the pop culture aspect and soaring value and was generally reported uncritically. This is opposed to what specialised sources were reporting,

which tended to be along the lines of: "This is a scam, don't buy it."

7. SQUID was not the first instance of this happening. Earlier in the same year, a crypto currency inspired by *The Mandalorian*, known as Mando, had done almost the exact same thing. They capitalised on the popularity of the Disney+ series to gain press coverage and make a lot of money. Then they made off with all of it.

The discerning investor would have noticed these signs and steered clear of SQUID. Unfortunately, many newcomers and amateurs were hoodwinked and lost their money. Do not allow this to happen to you.

Summary

Making money in the new financial system is not very different compared to traditional investments, and as such, most traditional investment advice applies. Ensure you understand what you are investing in, that you do not put all your eggs in one basket, that the asset is robust and easily tradeable, and that the wallets and exchanges that you make use of are secure. Always bear in mind that crypto assets are more vulnerable to scams and extreme, rapid fluctuations in value. Potential investors must be extra careful and ensure they know what they are doing. As much as investing early and being ahead of the curve can pay off in a big way, things can also go very wrong if you handle your money in an unsafe way. Always keep your wits about you, keep an eye out for red flags, and get your information from a variety of reliable sources.

Chapter 6:

Challenges for the New

Financial System

When we read about blockchain and cryptocurrency online and on social media, opinions tend to be polarised. Usually, you will find complete pessimists who see no potential benefits or improvements to the current system in the new systems. You will also find unchecked enthusiasts who see no potential flaws or dangers whatsoever. Both of these extremes are divorced from reality. The truth of the matter lies somewhere in the middle.

Up until now, we have spoken about the benefits and potential of the technologies taking our financial system in a bold new direction. However, it's not all sunshine and rainbows. There still some major flaws and obstacles in these new systems that prevent them from being fully viable as an alternative to our current system (for now).

Mining Constraints

While it is possible to obtain cryptocurrency without mining it, it cannot exist in the first place without mining. Recall our earlier discussions of Bitcoin. Miners are essential for every single transaction to take place, as they need to verify each new transaction. New Bitcoins are created as a reward for mining. So, even if you buy your Bitcoin on an exchange and do not mine it yourself, somebody else did. However, to preserve the value of the currency, mining becomes more and more difficult and requires more and more processing power. Mining a single Bitcoin when it was launched in 2009 could be done on a normal laptop. Nowadays, profiting from Bitcoin mining requires a powerful setup on an industrial scale. This might mean building a dedicated mining rig with multiple specialized processors, or it might mean installing crypto miners on multiple computers (note: doing so without permission constitutes voluntarily spreading of malware and is against the law in most countries). This poses a series of problems that are difficult to overcome.

Mining requires access to resources. You must have access to enough money to purchase the right equipment, and you must have access to that equipment. Considering the global shortages in the wafers used for manufacturing processors, that means it can be very difficult to obtain hardware, and much more expensive to do so. To remain profitable, miners always aim to mine faster than their competitors, which means they always need to be upgrading their hardware to the most efficient models. Effective mining requires significant start-up capital, which is pretty difficult to come by if you are not already rich. Credit providers tend to be hesitant to issue loans for crypto-mining purposes because the industry is so volatile. As such, loans tend to have high interest rates.

Furthermore, mining cryptocurrency (and the production of other crypto assets, such as NFT minting) uses a lot of energy. Mining setups require access to constant, affordable electricity. A mining setup in a country where electricity is very expensive or unreliable is unlikely to be profitable. This means that miners often need to resort to outsourcing their operations or setting up a network of mining machines in different locations. This, again, requires a lot of money, and unfortunately also often ties in with cybercrime and the spreading of malware. While the reliance on energy generation has led to mining operations constructing their own green power sources, such as solar panels, unfortunately, they do still make use of so-called "dirty" energy to an unsustainable degree.

Lastly, because the industry is so new, there is no rulebook on effectively running a mining operation long term. As such, access to knowledgeable staff is a rare luxury. There are almost no qualifications that focus specifically on cryptocurrency, blockchain, or crypto-mining, so industrial-scale mining operations must often make do with second-best, or otherwise be permanently short on competent staff.

Security

When it comes to cybersecurity, there is a very important maxim to bear in mind: anything can be hacked eventually. If something has access to the internet, no matter how secure it may be, it is not invulnerable. Anything that claims to be completely secure or "uncrackable" is inviting malicious actors to do their best to hack it. There is a good reason why the way that bot-detection software like Captcha works is constantly changing and is a closely guarded secret. Malicious actors are improving their techniques at the same rate that cyber-security experts are improving theirs.

The main vulnerability is not blockchain or cryptocurrency itself, but rather exchanges and wallets. In the previous chapter, we spoke a bit about the importance of using a secure wallet and complex passwords. However, there is always a factor of human error in any system, waiting to be discovered and exploited. The exchange you use might be breached, such as in the 2014 hack of the major crypto-exchange platform, Mt. Gox, which caused the whole site to shut down. Mt. Gox did not have proper version control systems and its internal development and source code was messy and poorly written. As such, it was a ticking time bomb. When the bomb went off, millions of US dollars' worth of Bitcoin were stolen from users' wallets (McMillan, 2014).

Even if the platform you use is totally secure as far as security experts can determine, there is always an element of the unknown. Undiscovered vulnerabilities in software have a way of being discovered by malicious actors before the alarm is raised. In 2021, a vulnerability in a widely used code library, known as Apache Log4j, was discovered. It had been present since the library was deployed in 2015 but had remained unknown and unexploited for six years (Srinivas & Sirsalewala, 2021). This library is so commonly used that it affected billions of programs and devices, including industrial equipment, video games, payroll software, and even major services like Amazon Web Services, which is used for roughly 34% of all websites (Underwood, 2021). Again, there is no way for the average user to know something like this.

In short, anything virtual has an inherent security risk and can theoretically be exploited. It might be argued that this is no different from, say, a bank robbery, but it is. There is a much greater physical risk to a bank robber than to a hacker, and as such, it is much easier to execute and get away with hacking. Furthermore, the pseudo-anonymity of cryptocurrencies compared to normal bank accounts, along with the irreversibility of transactions, makes it almost impossible to retrieve stolen crypto assets.

Impending Regulation

As new financial innovations become more prevalent and less of a niche hobby, they start to enter the realm of requiring regulation. Currently, crypto is largely unregulated, and the unregulated nature thereof is one of the main reasons many people are drawn to it. Unfortunately, this is unlikely to last. As countries begin to recognize the environmental impact of crypto-mining and the potential for abuse, more regulation is inevitable.

Already, Iran and China have issued bans on crypto mining within their borders, and other countries like Russia have proposed similar bans. Religious leaders have also spoken out against investing in crypto assets, likening it to gambling and urging it to be regulated. There are also issues regarding income tracing for tax and inheritance purposes, and concerns regarding tax evasion and the role of cryptocurrency in other criminal activities are becoming more prevalent.

Therefore, large-scale investment in cryptocurrency, such as through mining, is somewhat of a political risk. What do you do if your country outlaws your investment or your business? What happens if a large portion of the market loses interest because the "no regulations" selling point has disappeared?

That being said, while the unknown outcome of impending regulation is a challenge, the lack of regulation is a challenge in itself. An unregulated space lends itself to criminality, poor or no standardisation, and unchecked feuds between interest groups. Already the lack of standardised "bare minimum" security and privacy protocols has led to serious data breaches and theft. There are also no legal descriptions regarding key terminology, so there stands to be some abuse of terminology as selling points in the same way that the word "green" can be put on the packaging of any product without actually adhering to any eco-friendly standards.

The unregulated state of the system currently is a problem just as much as impending regulation will be a challenge.

Value Decline

This book has spoken at length about the volatility of crypto-assets and their value. This is because a crypto asset is entirely virtual, so its value is strongly tied to its perceived importance and value. In other words, it becomes more valuable based on how useful it is and how people perceive it. Spikes in cryptocurrencies' value are tied to headlines and media attention, which is one of the reasons SQUID became so valuable even though it was definitely not useful or promising. Even stable currencies like Bitcoin see spikes and crashes in their value depending on public opinion and perceived value.

While crypto is currently on the rise in perceived value and potential contribution to society, it has received an almost equal amount of criticism. As more people take advantage of community enthusiasm (especially enthusiasm uncoupled from financial literacy) and amateur investors lose their money, backlash and negative media attention may increase. As a result, the perceived usefulness and value of crypto assets in the public eye may decline, and the actual value thereof will decline with it.

In addition to a market value decline, this will also have an impact on miners. In order to survive a decline like this, mining operations need to be profitable enough to keep going even when returns are low. Due to the constraints mentioned earlier, this is not always possible, and a permanent decline would pose a bigger problem. Considering how reliant the new financial system would be on mining, this is quite a big risk.

Technological Limitations

As incredible and versatile as blockchain is, it does have its limitations, both in terms of hardware capacity and programming. Firstly, blockchain is essentially software, which means it was coded by a person or team of people. Human error is always a factor in software, no matter what. This can lead to vulnerabilities and security risks in the blockchain itself, not just the applications we use to interact with blockchains. Open source blockchain projects can reduce the human error factor by allowing people to check, improve, and contribute to the code. However, it is not always feasible or advisable for every project. It is also challenging to find people with the right experience and skillset to handle blockchain maintenance.

Secondly, blockchains are slow compared to other technological systems that fulfill similar roles, especially when thinking about scalability. While crypto trading is marketed as being very fast compared to trading systems that require third parties like banks, in reality, this is not always the case, as blockchain technology in itself is slower than centralised servers. A network of miners is required for any transaction to take place or a new block to be added to the ledger, and mining is an arduous, energy-intensive process. As such, any changes to the blockchain can take several days to process and complete, meaning transactions can take much longer than they would if they were using other platforms. This problem compounds when more users come into play. Blockchains have significant performance issues when too many people are using the same blockchain at once, making them cumbersome and inefficient at a large scale. However, blockchains require a large community of miners to function efficiently and thus end up in a feedback loop of needing more users but not being able to sustain more users. In order for large-scale adoption of blockchain technology to work or for it to become mainstream in the financial system, this efficiency and scaling issue must be addressed somehow.

Trade Barriers

Crypto trading in itself has multiple issues that need to be addressed. Again, there is the issue of security. The large number of rip off merchants that make use of crypto trading to steal money and the inability to track down and bring criminals to justice also causes issues, especially when it can be hard for newcomers to spot when a new project is illegitimate. The prevalence of illegitimate crypto products diminishes the credibility of the sector as a whole, bringing down the value of crypto-currencies and discouraging new investors.

Secondly, crypto trading can have high transaction fees. Despite claims that cryptocurrency transactions have low fees, this is usually not the case. Transaction fees can be high, and in some cases fees that are too low may even discourage miners from verifying transactions, meaning that transactions will sometimes get "stuck" for several days. This further contributes to the overall potential for slowness of crypto trading.

Lastly, crypto markets tend to have variable or even low liquidity. This means that crypto-assets can be difficult to trade without decreasing value and causing the market to become even more volatile than it already is. Some exchanges, like Binance, put measures in place to increase liquidity on their platform, but this, in turn, raises transaction fees. Unfortunately, if any platform has lower liquidity than another, a power imbalance arises in which platforms with higher liquidity can manipulate prices and raise their listing fees to an unreasonable amount.

Digital Divide

The digital divide refers to the gap in access to technology between developed and less developed countries. Less developed countries tend to have less access to infrastructure and advanced technology, especially in rural areas, than developed countries. The gap can also be replicated on a smaller scale between big cities and rural areas, and even across income groups.

While mobile phones and wireless technology are making significant progress in providing equal access to the internet and electronic services, the scale of literacy and types of technology that is required to have universal access to crypto-assets and new financial systems is more difficult to bridge. Even traditional finance is still struggling to bridge this gap and improve financial inclusion rates.

Currently, traditional banks have bricks-and-mortar branches, websites, apps, and phone banking services that do not require a smartphone. Crypto does not have this sort of range. You need access to the internet, and therefore at least a decent smartphone, to even acquire crypto in the first place. The literacy requirements to safely trade crypto is also much higher, and people with less access to information are more likely to fall victim to extortion, theft, and scams.

Metaverse becomes even more problematic than crypto assets. As we'll see in the next chapter, the metaverse will be heavily reliant on constant internet connectivity and access to advanced devices. It has a strong virtual reality (VR) and augmented reality (AR) component, and therefore will likely require devices that are simply not economically viable for many — if not most — people. Furthermore, the Internet of Things component of metaverse also requires significant upfront investment and infrastructural development that is simply not viable when many devices are not even available for purchase, let alone purchase at an affordable price, in many countries.

In conclusion, the new financial sector has some significant obstacles that need to be overcome before it can truly become mainstream, but that is not to say that it is inherently problematic. Like any new industry, it will take a while for things to fully normalise and for all the kinks to be worked out. Any system has flaws, especially new systems. However, when the dust has settled, the new financial system should have fewer flaws than the current financial system.

Summary

Before we can expect the future financial system to become our present financial system, some major obstacles need to be cleared first. These obstacles include barriers to large-scale mining, as well as what could happen in the event of insufficient mining, software limitations regarding the speed and efficiency of blockchain technology, declining value and unstable markets, potential security risks and scams, and the present uncertainty regarding regulations.

Chapter 7:

Metaverse — Emergence

and Significance

Holograms, teleportation, virtual reality, augmented reality, everything connected and lightning fast. It sounds like something from science fiction, but it won't be for much longer. Metaverse enthusiasts believe the metaverse will challenge the current state of the internet for the better. This chapter looks at what we can expect from the metaverse, why it is important, and how it will impact our financial system.

Emergence

The metaverse has evolved over a number of decades, with more room for growth. As the ubiquity of the internet and access to smart devices grows, we become closer to living in a metaverse. Earlier, we likened any fully digital social space, especially ones modeled after real-life societies, to the metaverse. This is a really useful way to think of a metaverse and conceptualise what a fully digital, online society might look like. However, the recent trend in companies recalibrating themselves to focus on the metaverse (such as Facebook rebranding as Meta) is heralding a different understanding of the metaverse. Rather than entering a separate metaverse, we would exist within the metaverse at the same time as our "regular" universe.

Currently, no matter how connected we are and how interconnected our devices and accounts are, the internet and our digital spaces are still something that we deliberately visit, not something that is all around us. To enter a digital society, as in our *ArcheAge* example a couple of chapters ago, we must go to our computer and log on. To check social media, we must open the relevant apps or websites. Virtual spaces are still a sort of "secondary location" but gradually, our understanding of this is changing and it could well be that entering virtual spaces in the near future would be a matter of putting on a pair of glasses in the morning (or something similar to that).

Currently, Virtual Reality (VR) and Augmented Reality (AR) are still limited to entertainment in many ways. VR headsets are usually designed with gaming or watching movies in mind. AR is usually applied to the world via camera lenses and is still impractical in ordinary situations. However, the rapid shift to remote work and digital hangouts with friends and family which was forced by the start of the COVID-19 pandemic has pushed people and companies to begin to explore the possibilities. For example, work that requires multiple monitors may become cumbersome in a home environment, which can be easily remedied by using a VR headset to project multiple monitors into thin air. No more pets and children blocking your view and knocking over important devices. Nobody can look at what you are doing over your shoulder.

Meta CEO, Mark Zuckerberg, explained at the conference where he announced the Facebook rebrand into Meta that the metaverse he envisions is not one in which his company is a monopoly, or a universe purely for socialisation and entertainment. Rather, he envisioned a world in which everything we do is digitised in some way or at least has some virtual component to it. He used the examples of "teleporting" to meetings by having a hologram of you projected in a boardroom while you are participating remotely, or projected screens instead of physical ones, or ownership of digital assets.

It is this final category that is of most interest to many of us interested in the future of the financial world, but that is not the only thing that will be relevant to blockchain and crypto enthusiasts.

Significance

Building the metaverse is significant both within and outside of the financial sector. Outside of our finances, the most important things that an expansive metaverse will achieve is the enrichment of relationships and the further breakdown of global barriers. Historically, people have been bound by geography. People who prioritise their jobs may need to move away from friends and family, have long and expensive commutes, or travel frequently. People who prioritise their social ties are limited in career prospects and access to amenities, infrastructure, and resources. In times of isolation, such as during the pandemic, these limitations become even more pronounced. However, with improvements in technology and digital communications, we have been able to remain connected and work remotely. Adding in further developments in AR and VR can make it feel like we are actually right there with our friends and family, even when we are apart. We can be present at any office in the world without being limited by transportation, isolation, or borders. We will no longer need to choose between social lives and career opportunities, we can do both remotely.

Financially, we can expect the expansion of the digital asset class and further developments of fully online businesses, such as NFT merchants and avatar designers. We can also expect more businesses that enrich our online spaces and make them feel more alive, more dapps, and more DAOs. By extension, we can expect an increase in the usability, usefulness, and prevalence of cryptocurrency and crypto trading.

However, the expansion of digital assets and stabilisation of cryptocurrencies is not the only important piece here. We also need to consider the state of the internet. As it stands, online privacy is eroding and most of what we do online requires going through a handful of mega corporations with iron grips on the tech sector, such as Google, Apple, Meta, Twitter, and Microsoft. In other words, the internet is becoming increasingly centralised and is losing its anonymity. In part, this is why so many people are interested in blockchain and its inherent privacy and decentralisation. In order for the metaverse to be successful, the issues with the current internet need to be addressed, and the backbone of crypto is just the way to do it.

Building Blocks of the Metaverse

The metaverse is not a single technology, and therefore cannot be built in isolation. The development of the metaverse requires the further development of some important technologies concurrently. The most important facets that contribute to the metaverse are Web 3.0, virtual and augmented reality, and blockchain.

Web 3.0

The metaverse will rely on the development of Web 3.0, which is intertwined with greater integration of blockchain technology. To understand why that is, let's have a look at how the iterations of the internet as we know it have progressed and what we can expect from Web 3.0.

Web 1.0 was the first iteration and consisted of mostly static pages that people could view, but not really interact with. It can be described as the "read-only" internet. You create your website, put it online, and people view it. If something changes, you change the website itself.

Web 2.0 is an evolved version of Web 1.0 and is what our current internet resembles. This is a read-write, highly interactive version of the internet. Websites become apps and platforms with live feeds and user-generated content. Sites like Reddit and TikTok and online shopping sites have become the norm. Anyone can create their own sites with platforms like WordPress. However, this has brought us to a dilemma where the internet is reliant on companies that provide platforms, and the bigger those companies become, the more problematic that is for online freedom and privacy. Facebook and YouTube both famously boost controversial and potentially dangerous content to promote user engagement. Apple's content policies for advertisements have forced sites like Tumblr to censor their users and ban content to avoid removal from Apple's App Store. Dedication to advertisement revenue has caused companies to steer their business models towards "marketable" material, burying content by marginalised users and creators.

Web 3.0 addresses the issues of Web 2.0 by returning to the original model of the internet as a private, decentralised space. While some of its aspects are geared towards improvements in marketing and corporate presence online, much of its building blocks will undo the creeping centralisation of the internet.

Web 3.0 is characterised by five key things. Firstly, and most importantly for blockchain, Web 3.0 is decentralised. With the prominence of blockchain technology and interest in privacy and decentralisation, especially outside of financial applications, more decentralised and blockchain-based services and spaces are emerging. We can expect less identity verification, more diversity in services, more equality and neutrality, and fewer monopolies. While this requires more interest and investment in blockchain, it will feed the viability of blockchain in more and more sectors. Web 3.0 is likely to be permissionless, verifiable, trustless, and self-governing as a direct response to the current state of Web 2.0.

Secondly, Web 3.0 will be ubiquitous, meaning it will be everywhere. This is where it most obviously connects with metaverse concepts. You will be able to access Web 3.0 anywhere, at any time. Any given service, platform, or website would need to be adaptable to any device. Internet of Things will also have a big role to play in this aspect of Web 3.0. Imagine trading Bitcoin from an app on your smart fridge while you think about what you want out of the fridge for breakfast! By integrating online activities thoroughly into our daily and physical lives, we are building both the metaverse and Web 3.0.

Thirdly, Web 3.0 will involve 3D graphics and interfaces. Again, this connects with the metaverse.

Web 3.0 will involve online identities that are just as important as our offline identities and immersing ourselves in worlds that are beyond the physical one. VR and AR will be more integrated into our use of the internet; our online spaces will manifest in our physical spaces. There is a very clear overlap between what we can expect from Web 3.0 and what we can expect from the metaverse.

Fourthly, we can expect more use of artificial intelligence (AI) in our technology. We can expect more and better smart assistants like Amazon's Alexa and Microsoft's Cortana, semi-autonomous and even fully autonomous vehicles, support bots, and home robots. These are all spectacular and show-stopping examples of AI, but we will also see more mundane AI. One of the most important uses for AI is in data analysis. Computers can do maths better and faster than humans can, but without AI we can't really use them for pattern recognition or making meaningful deductions from large quantities of data - that required humans. Now, however, we are starting to use AI more and more to analyse data for more effective marketing and suggestions for users.

If you've ever thought you might be interested in buying something, only for that to appear as an advertisement on your social media feed, that's AI in action! Your phone isn't listening to your thoughts, companies are using AIs to make super accurate predictions of what you might be interested in based on past purchases, the apps you download, your age bracket, your search history, your gender, and your engagement with interests online. A bit creepy, but it's all data that you allow websites to collect by allowing cookies, trackers, and signing in with the same accounts everywhere. Now, while we can expect even further expansion of AI in this way (among other ways), we can also expect these analyses to be less invasive. As mentioned earlier, we're seeing a big movement towards increased privacy and decentralisation, even in terms of government regulation, so companies will need to adapt their strategies to be less surveillance-based.

Lastly, Web 3.0 will be more human. The whole concept of Web 3.0 was inspired by the idea of the "Semantic Web," in which our computers will understand us just as well as other people can. Computers don't really understand that there is no difference between "I am financially literate" and "I have financial literacy." They mean the same thing to a person, but a computer relies on syntax to understand, and the difference in syntax may result in very different outcomes. Web 3.0 would eliminate this issue by creating a way for computers to understand semantics as a person can.

Combining these five aspects, we can see how Web 3.0 and the metaverse overlap. Both of them involve decentralisation, smarter devices and more presence in our daily lives. Web 3.0 is essential in building the metaverse.

Virtual and Augmented Reality

Virtual reality (VR) refers to technology that allows us to immerse ourselves in digital worlds, using 3D graphics and allowing us to interact with objects and people in that digital world as though it was real life. Currently, it is mostly used for video games, allowing players to feel as though they are really in that game's world. VR can also be used to add a sense of depth and immersion to films and videos, making them feel more alive and interactive by allowing the viewer to change their own perspective of a scene by moving around.

However, companies like Meta are looking to expand VR to become a social tool, allowing us to interact with our friends and family in 3D spaces. Others are working on VR applications for live events (attend a concert or match without actually being there), therapy (receive exposure therapy without having to physically be exposed to something terrifying or dangerous), education (medical students can practice surgery risk-free), and accessible tourism (take a trip somewhere even if you can't afford the real thing). Even now, people are using VR spaces for work, allowing them to have multiple monitors without actually needing the space and hardware to have it physically exist. We can expect this to develop even further, eventually becoming a norm for desk jobs.

Augmented reality (AR) adds virtual elements to the real world. Currently, this is mostly applied via cameras, usually using a smartphone or other mobile device. The virtual elements aren't actually manifesting around us. However, as AR devices like Magic Leap become more affordable and commonplace, we can expect to see more ways to enhance reality that doesn't require us to view it through a camera. Instead, wearing a headset or pair of goggles will allow us to see virtual elements in the real world. AR can also refer to holograms and projections that make it seem like virtual graphics are actually present in the real world, even without us needing our own devices. We are already seeing this in eye-catching displays like the incredibly realistic dragon used at the 2017 League of Legends World Championship, but we can also expect holograms to make an appearance in our ordinary lives.

The metaverse relies on VR and AR to make digital worlds integrate into our physical world, making it more connected and virtual without requiring us to view the virtual world as a "secondary location." It will also allow us to enter digital spaces and be more fully immersed. The metaverse looks to essentially blur the lines between what is "real" and what is "digital" by making the digital more real, becoming just as important to us as the physical world.

Blockchain

For the metaverse to be viable, something needs to be done about the major public backlash against IoT, tech monopolies, and surveillance. One of the best ways to do this is to make use of the facilities offered by blockchains to improve privacy and decentralise the internet. Considering that a fully realised metaverse will have online assets, finance, objects, properties, and more, it is crucial to have a secure and private way to keep track of who owns what, and blockchain can fulfill that role through decentralised ledgers.

Blockchain can also be used to automate legal agreements through smart contracts. Smart contracts are bits of code that run on blockchains that essentially work on the principle of "if this then that." They can be used to automate the enforcement of legal agreements and ensure these agreements cannot be altered or tampered with. Well-written smart contracts can be used to automate ownership and form the basis of DAOs.

A further increase in online shopping and remote work will also foster effective payment systems which are secure and unaffected by foreign exchange rates. Cryptocurrencies and blockchain can fulfill this role as well. This would require the technology and currencies to stabilise a bit more, but that is already in the works.

Lastly, blockchain is a necessary part of NFTs. As we move to a more digital world, we can expect NFTs to be more commonplace. Currently, NFTs are mostly used for art, but as ownership of digital assets gains prevalence, we might use NFTs to purchase accessories for digital avatars or digital objects. In order to ensure that the creators and businesses we buy from do not defraud us, these assets can be stored as NFTs, ensuring that we will always own the things we paid for (unless a smart contract, for example, was to include a repossession clause).

Currently, the only way to avoid surveillance online is to take extreme privacy measures or simply not participate. In the age of the metaverse, refusing to participate will be less of an option, and taking extreme privacy measures may become less and less feasible the more ubiquitous online technology becomes. Therefore, using secure, decentralised, and private systems such as blockchain will become absolutely crucial.

Digital Assets

The metaverse seeks to digitise most of our assets, meaning the things we own will be digital, and our ownership of these things will be proven through digital means. We have already discussed how blocks on a blockchain can represent anything, not just records or financial transactions, but let's dive into that a bit more. Up until now, we haven't really spoken about NFTs other than mentioning that they exist and that they are a type of digital asset you can trade, buy, and invest in. At present, NFTs are mostly used to trade art and unique avatars or cosmetic items in online worlds. However, an NFT can be much more than that.

Before we continue, let's clarify some terminology. An NFT is a non-fungible token. "Fungible" is an economic term referring to how easy it is to trade an asset. Currency or physical assets like gold are fungible.

Any GBP pound is worth exactly the same as another. They are interchangeable. The same goes for gold. Any two bars of gold that are the same weight have the same value and are interchangeable. Fungible assets can be traded at many exchanges fairly easily (Milton, 2021). If I have 200 stocks in Apple that I bought from the London Stock Exchange, I can go to any other stock exchange and sell them there for whatever they are currently worth. Fungibility is defined by whether you can buy a given amount of an asset, then sell the same amount of the asset, and end up with nothing (except hopefully a profit). If I sell my 200 stocks in Apple, I will have zero stocks in Apple, and whatever profits I have made.

This principle of fungibility also applies to currency — both fiat and crypto. If you travel abroad, you trade the currency you have for the currency you want, ending up with the same amount of currency — a net-zero exchange. If I have $10 for example and want to travel to Europe, I need to purchase Euros. Assuming the exchange rate is 0.5 USD to 1 EUR, my $10 will be worth €5. When I return, my €5 can be converted back to $10 (assuming the exchange rate is the same). Thus, a net-zero transaction with the possibility of profit or loss, depending on the fluctuation of value dependent on the exchange rate.

NFTs are non-fungible. Meaning one NFT cannot be exchanged for another NFT, or any asset of a similar value, in a net-zero transaction. If I have an NFT worth 1 BTC, and I sell it for 1.1 BTC, I will have made a profit of 0.1 BTC, but I will no longer have an asset.

This makes trading NFTs less similar to stock trading or ForEx investment, and more similar to a property market investment. If I have a plot of land that I sell, I may turn a profit, but I will no longer have the land. That is not a bad thing, and it doesn't mean that trading non-fungible assets is bad, it just means that the transaction is not net-zero. After all, the point of investing is to turn a profit, not to ensure all transactions are net-zero.

An NFT consists of two parts. Firstly, a digital asset that you can buy and sell, and secondly, a record of ownership. NFTs are created or "minted" in a similar way to how cryptocurrency is mined. Calculations are performed, producing a unique token that represents a block on the blockchain. That block contains information showing who owns the accompanying digital asset.

NFTs have drawn significant criticism, usually along the lines of suggesting that someone who owns an NFT does not actually own the asset they bought, merely proof of ownership of that asset. In the case of art, why buy an NFT when you can simply commission an artist to create something for you? The answer lies in the proof of ownership. When you commission digital art, the artist sends you the file you paid for, but there is no unalterable record of ownership. The artist could, theoretically, continue to sell copies of that artwork. Perhaps this does not seem like an issue at first glance but imagine if we did that with other assets. Without a deed proving that it belongs to you, how could you prevent trespassing, vandalism, and illegal occupation of your property or land? Without proof of ownership of a vehicle, how could you report its theft to the police? Would it even be theft if you could not prove it belongs to you? If your ownership of an asset came into question, how could you verify it if you did not have any proof of purchase?

The real power of NFTs is not so much in their current use in the art world, but in the metaverse. When more of our assets are digitised, we will need unalterable proof of ownership. If I were to purchase a digital home, I would need a deed for that home. However, traditional systems and databases can be altered or tampered with, so it is important to have a transparent record proving my ownership. Therefore, we need the blockchain to produce NFTs so that we can have digital assets.

A lot of the criticism leveled at digital assets has to do with how "real" the value of a digital asset is. With something like cryptocurrency, the value is partially determined by public opinion. When public opinion does not view a fully digital asset as a "real" asset, it lacks value. However, the distinction between physical and digital assets is continually eroding, and in a perfectly integrated global metaverse, the distinction will be so blurred as to be practically non-existent.

There are obviously some assets that cannot be fully digitised. People still have physical bodies, and therefore have physical needs. The point of the metaverse and NFTs is not to eliminate the physical world, but to enhance it. You could have a physical home but trade your physical transportation for "teleporting" to a virtual office. This further opens up the possibilities. If I own a virtual vacation home in a scenic virtual reality, I could rent it out or create a timeshare. This could be managed through dapps (something similar to Airbnb, for example), DAOs (such as resort membership organisations), or even smart contracts to automate a lease agreement. After all, the digital world will become just as important and "tangible" as the real one in the metaverse, so why should it be more limited? The point of the metaverse is to remove limitations!

Metaverse Startups? Metaverse Tokens?

Currently, there is no one unified metaverse that is integrated into everyone's daily lives, but smaller metaverses that we willingly enter do exist and are on the rise. Within these metaverses, in-universe currencies exist, and given the blockchain bases of modern metaverses, these are often cryptocurrencies. Thus, a metaverse token is a cryptocurrency belonging to a given metaverse. Metaverse tokens can be grouped under the blockchain functions required for a fully realised metaverse, but it can be a bit confusing to do so, which is why we are discussing them separately.

When you look up "metaverse" or "metaverse blockchain" you may find some results about various coins and start-ups with metaverse in their name. These are examples of metaverse tokens (cryptocurrencies), self-contained metaverses, and companies that are focused on contributing to building the global metaverse. These must be differentiated from "the metaverse" as we are referring to in this book. Singular elements of a metaverse are not the same as the ubiquitous, fully integrated metaverse. There is likely not going to be a single "metaverse token" or currency used by the whole metaverse, just as Bitcoin is not the only cryptocurrency and GBP pounds are not the only fiat currency.

Barriers

We cannot expect a fully realised metaverse any time soon, but we can expect more and more elements of metaverse technology to be implemented in our daily lives. In other words, while we can't expect all the building blocks we discussed to be fully integrated into society, we can expect more self-contained metaverses, more implementations of blockchain, more development towards Web 3.0, more digital assets, more fully online communities, and businesses, and more improvements to VR and AR technology. For the universal metaverse to become a reality, there are still many barriers that need to be overcome, including cost, technological limitations, public opinion, and income disparities.

Cost

The most significant barrier to implementation is cost. IoT devices, VR headsets, AR projectors, and AR goggles are currently very expensive and not widely available. There are only a few options on the market, all of which cost a pretty penny. There are cheaper options, such as headsets that use a smartphone and blinders to create a sense of VR, but these are only really useful for watching videos or exploring virtual spaces without interacting with anything. These won't work well for the fully interactive, 3D virtual spaces that will define the metaverse.

A metaverse requires all members to have some way of accessing and interacting with it. With a self-contained metaverse, membership is optional, and the basic access requirement is not a big stumbling block. However, a fully integrated metaverse that everyone participates in will require significant investment. This will likely involve infrastructure development, corporate investment, more alternatives and cost-effective products on the market, and personal buy-in. As with the invention of personal computers in the 1980s, it will take a while before this technology becomes essential to almost everyone.

Technological Limitations

The metaverse is limited by the hardware and software that apply to VR, AR, IoT, and AI. All of these things require processing power, expensive hardware, substantial infrastructure, and well-written software. Each of these is limited by knowledge, cost, and availability of materials.

As an example, crypto mining requires significant processing power. Material shortages contributing to an overall shortage of processors, as well as steadily slowing progress in developing faster, more powerful processors, are creating entry barriers to mining that makes it difficult and expensive to mine effectively while turning a profit. Each element of the metaverse has similar technological issues to overcome.

Income Inequality

Self-contained metaverses (and small-scale implementations of metaverse technologies) do exist already, but participation is limited by access to resources and infrastructure. We've already spoken about the costs associated with developing and acquiring the technology required for a proper metaverse to exist, but this section is less about overall costs and more about delays in large-scale adoption.

We can expect the metaverse to be delayed in implementation and accessibility because of income. Less developed countries, rural areas, and low-income communities will likely not see access until quite a while after adoption in developed countries, urban areas, and high-income communities. Historically, there has been a significant lag in technology and development along income lines, contributing to the digital divide we spoke about earlier. When many people don't have access to high-speed internet (or any internet at all), lack stable electrical connections, and their access to technology is mostly restricted to mobile phones, we can't really expect a global, fully integrated metaverse.

High- and middle-income people who live in areas with sufficient infrastructure will likely experience the metaverse first, just as they were the first to experience self-contained metaverses and the first to become involved in crypto-trading. After all, investment in new technologies and crypto-currency requires upfront financial buy-in, which low-income people simply do not have. Income inequality poses a significant barrier to a global metaverse.

Metaverse Investment

Investing in the metaverse can be compared to investing in early tech startups when the internet and personal computers were still brand new. We don't know what exactly we can expect, but we know it's going to be big, and we know our financial world will depend on it both for income and infrastructure as it becomes more prevalent. Investing in the metaverse now will put you ahead of the curve. Below is a non-exhaustive list of some opportunities to get financially involved in the future.

Firstly, you could invest in businesses that are actively building the metaverse. This is just traditional stock trading, but it puts you ahead of the curve, similar to people who invested in tech startups in the 1980s and 1990s. Secondly, any investment in blockchain-based technologies and cryptocurrency contributes to the growth of the industry and further development of technology. Lastly, you could invest in virtual world tokens. In other words, buy some sort of stake in self-contained metaverses, usually through a form of crypto-currency or NFT. This could be a parcel of virtual land or digital collectibles in a game world.

Regardless of how you choose to invest in the metaverse, investing in this new aspect of our financial future is similar to investing in other aspects: high risk, high reward. Not all companies will succeed, and not everything that claims to be the next big thing is going to make good on that promise. We want to avoid being the next Ronals Wayne (remember him from chapter 1?), but we also want to avoid making rash decisions that can cost us our "real world" wealth or livelihoods. Be sure to keep your newfound knowledge in mind and make informed decisions with your physical and digital assets.

Summary

The metaverse is vast, and it can be difficult to keep track of what people mean when they say "metaverse."

A fully integrated metaverse that is accessible from anywhere in the world at any point in time is likely quite far off. But the gradual integration of Web 3.0, AR and VR, various digital assets, and blockchain technology into our daily lives is already happening. We are seeing more and more applications of blockchain technology and innovative uses for NFTs every day. Self-contained metaverses are multiplying and deepening in complexity, involving more and more crypto-assets and implementations of blockchain. We can get ahead of the curve by investing in businesses that are actively contributing to building a comprehensive and safe metaverse, and by trading metaverse tokens and other crypto assets. However, there are some serious obstacles that need to be overcome before the metaverse can become more than just a novelty for tech enthusiasts and high-income groups. These obstacles include inequality, cost, and technological limitations.

Conclusion:

A New Kind of Financial

Literacy

In reading this book, you have already taken a bold step toward the future. Your financial literacy and preparedness for the future have markedly improved. You now have a solid understanding of the components that form the foundations of our future financial world. Even while new technologies develop and we wait for the dust to settle, we can rely on the foundations this book has discussed.

Through our discussion on Bitcoin, you understand alternatives to fiat money and commercial banking. Through blockchain and Ethereum, you understand security and transparency. Through the metaverse, you understand the importance of the increasing digitisation of all our assets. You also have a picture of how wealth is created in this new system and have a good starting point for creating your own wealth. Lastly, you understand that this system, much like any other financial system or new phase in digital technology that came before it, is not without its flaws and challenges. There is no such thing as a perfect financial system.

However, we can extract the most benefit out of any system we find ourselves in by ensuring that we are equipped with the necessary knowledge.

If all these futuristic technologies and changes still seem quite strange or novel, even now that you understand all the key concepts, try to remember that the main thing that is changing is not the economy itself, but the technology we use to run it. The hardest part is usually just trying to wrap your head around the technological aspect, and once you've done that, you're halfway there!

As smart as humans are, we aren't *that* smart. History, and by extension our economic systems, tend to move in quite cyclical patterns. The future financial system replicates and builds upon existing structures. Trading cryptocurrency is not so different from trading foreign currencies, using a crypto-wallet is not so different from e-wallets. We can trace this pattern of incrementally improving our existing structures right back to the earliest human economies. Ultimately, we are simply fixing the holes and flaws in the current system. When the barter system proved to have trouble determining value, we invented currency. When fixed exchange rates and the gold standard led to the American stock market crash in the 1920s, we created flexible exchange rates to try and isolate economic crises. In 2009, in the aftermath of the biggest economic crisis since the Great Depression, we invented a new currency that did not require reliance on the institutions that let us down. Our financial system has undergone significant changes, and this is only the latest one.

It is important not to brush off the significance of the changes happening to the financial world. It may not impact you now, but it will, and sooner than you may think. Even the metaverse, which has some serious barriers to overcome, is not as far away as it might seem. This is why it is so important to equip yourself with an understanding of the basic principles underscoring our future financial system. There is a lot of panic and misinformation in the media, and it can be difficult to know what is going on at any given point in time — hence the importance of sound financial literacy.

The extent of your literacy in the new system will have a direct bearing on your future wealth. Those who understand the fundamentals of the changes that are happening and take the time to learn more and safely invest a bit will have a head start. You can compare it to stockbrokers in our current system. A stockbroker has deep knowledge of the current financial system, and they use that to their advantage. As a result, stockbrokers tend to be quite wealthy. Developing your knowledge about the future system will have a similar effect on you.

I encourage you to keep learning and keep discussing it with others. This field is rapidly evolving, with new information and developments emerging every day. Staying on top of new developments and collaborating with others to deepen your understanding is crucial to remaining literate. Just as a doctor must continuously attend seminars and stay up to date on new treatments, the financially literate person must do the same for new economic and technological developments. Remember that this knowledge is not just beneficial, it is essential in the same way that understanding interest rates are essential to getting credit. The current financial system is approaching serious upheaval, and soon. You must be prepared for it.

Do's and Don'ts After Reading

DO read more about cryptocurrency, blockchain, and the metaverse. Learn as much as you can from as many different sources as you can but be sure that all your sources are reliable. Avoid misinformation and echo chambers.

DO speak with your friends, family, colleagues, and even some experts about the new financial system and related technologies. Get many different viewpoints and opinions on these developments and share your literacy with others.

DO try your hand at investing in crypto assets like NFTs and cryptocurrencies, as well as some metaverse investments.

DON'T fall for scams. Remember that many people are taking advantage of the excitement surrounding new technological developments to make their fortunes by defrauding amateur investors. There is no way to retrieve lost digital assets, so ensure that you stay safe.

DON'T make rash decisions. The markets are still volatile, so understand that investing in digital assets is currently high-risk, though this is likely to stabilise as the metaverse and other financial technologies mature.

DON'T spread misinformation or engage with articles and opinions uncritically. Doing so contributes to volatility in value and may lead less financially literate people to lose their money or make unsafe decisions. It also encourages more bad actors to attempt to take advantage of newcomers.

Above all, be ready for the future. Expand your literacy and knowledge, encourage others to do the same, and start building your future wealth. At present, physical wealth still takes priority, but as the metaverse expands and digital assets become more prevalent, this will begin to change. You are now ahead of the curve.

References

Afreen, S. (2021, September 8). *Why is Blockchain Important and Why Does it Matter.* Simplilearn.Com. https://www.simplilearn.com/tutorials/blockchain-tutorial/why-is-blockchain-important

Akram, H. (2019). *4 Issues Facing Cryptocurrency Today.* https://www.darwinrecruitment.com/blog/2018/02/big-issues-cryptocurrency-today

Aratani, L. (2021, November 1). Squid Game cryptocurrency collapses in apparent scam. *The Guardian.* https://www.theguardian.com/technology/2021/nov/01/squid-game-cryptocurrency-scam-fears-investors

Balaam, D. N., & Dillman, B. (2016). Chapter 7: The International Finance and Monetary Structure. In *Introduction to International Political Economy* (6th ed., pp. 151–177). Routledge.

Bansgopaul, N. (2021, September 15). *What Is Web 3.0 and Why Should You Care?* https://www.msn.com/en-us/news/technology/what-is-web-3-0-and-why-should-you-care/ar-AAOtjYM

Binance. (2021, December 6). *Metaverse Tokens: What, Why and How To Buy Them*. Binance Blog. https://www.binance.com/en/blog/fiat/met averse-tokens-what-why-and-how-to-buy-them-421499824684903124

Bitcoin. (n.d.). *What is Bitcoin? | How Do Bitcoin and Crypto Work?* Retrieved January 11, 2022, from https://www.bitcoin.com/get-started/what-is-bitcoin/

Bitcoin. (2018, August 24). *Myths—Bitcoin Wiki*. https://en.bitcoin.it/wiki/Myths#Bitcoin_is_just_like_all_other_digital_currencies.3B_noth ing_new

Blockchain.com Support. (2021, May 2). *Rejected Transactions*. Blockchain Support Center. https://support.blockchain.com/hc/en-us/articles/360018083772-Rejected-Transactions

Board of Governors of the Federal Reserve System. (n.d.). *What is the purpose of the Federal Reserve System?* Board of Governors of the Federal Reserve System. Retrieved January 11, 2022, from https://www.federalreserve.gov/faqs/about_12594.htm

Bry, A. (2022, January 7). *This Apple Co-Founder Sold His Stake For $800: How Much Would It Be Worth Now?* https://www.msn.com/en-us/money/news/this-apple-co-founder-sold-his-stake-for-24800-how-much-would-it-be-worth-now/ar-AASxISH

Burniske, C., & Tatar, J. (2017). *Cryptoassets: The Innovative Investor's Guide to Bitcoin and Beyond Hardcover* (1st ed.). McGraw Hill.

Business, J. V., CNN. (n.d.). *Squid Game crypto plunges to $0 after scammers steal millions of dollars from investors.* CNN. Retrieved January 12, 2022, from https://www.cnn.com/2021/11/01/investing/squid-game-cryptocurrency-scam/index.html

Bylund, A., & Speights, K. (2021, December 12). *Better Buy: Bitcoin vs. Ethereum.* The Motley Fool. https://www.fool.com/investing/2021/12/12/better-buy-bitcoin-vs-ethereum/

Cassiopeia Services. (2019, February 28). Challenges and issues in cryptocurrency trading: Beyond the controversies. *Medium.* https://cassiopeiaservicesltd.medium.com/challenges-and-issues-in-cryptocurrency-trading-beyond-the-controversies-12bebb7c3849

Chaum, D. L. (1982). *Computer Systems Established, Maintained and Trusted by Mutually Suspicious Groups.* University of California.

Clark, P. A. (2021, November 15). *The Metaverse Has Already Arrived. Here's What That Actually Means.* Time. https://time.com/6116826/what-is-the-metaverse/

Coinguides. (2019, May 17). What is a Bitcoin address, why is it important & how to get a BTC address? *Coin Guides.* https://coinguides.org/bitcoin-address-explained/

Colocation America. (2017, December 19). A Timeline of Net Neutrality in the United States and What It All Means. *Colocation America.* https://www.colocationamerica.com/blog/net-neutrality-timeline

Corporate Finance Institute. (2022). *Asset Class.* Corporate Finance Institute. https://corporatefinanceinstitute.com/resources/knowledge/trading-investing/asset-class/

Cuomo, J., Nash, R., Pureswaran, V., Thurlow, A., & Zaharchuk, D. (2017). *Building trust in government—Exploring the potential of blockchains.* IBM Institute for Business Value. https://www.ibm.com/downloads/cas/WJNPLNGZ

Dicken, P. (2015). *Global Shift Seventh Edition: Mapping the Changing Contours of the World Economy.* The Guilford Press.

Dixon, B. (2021, October 2). *Here's Why Bitcoin Is Still The Best Cryptocurrency To Invest In—E-Crypto News.* https://e-cryptonews.com/heres-why-bitcoin-is-still-the-best-cryptocurrency-to-invest-in/

Dredge, S. (2016, November 10). The complete guide to virtual reality – everything you need to get started. *The Guardian.* https://www.theguardian.com/technology/2016/nov/10/virtual-reality-guide-headsets-apps-games-vr

Duino, S. (2018, February 20). *What is Blockchain and why is it important?* https://medium.com/predict/what-is-blockchain-and-why-it-is-important-b341e3424893

Elliott, F. (2009, January 3). Chancellor Alistair Darling on brink of second bailout for banks. *The Times.* https://www.thetimes.co.uk/article/chancellor-alistair-darling-on-brink-of-second-bailout-for-banks-n9l382mn62h

Ely, A. (2021, October 10). What Is the Metaverse? Why Is it Important? *SimpleMoneyLyfe.*

https://simplemoneylyfe.com/what-is-the-metaverse/

Fintech News Hong Kong. (2021, September 14). What Is The Metaverse and Why is the Financial Sector Embracing It. *Fintech Hong Kong.* https://fintechnews.hk/16875/blockchain/what-is-the-metaverse-and-why-is-the-financial-sector-embracing-it/

Folger, J. (2021, October 28). *Metaverse.* Investopedia. https://www.investopedia.com/metaverse-definition-5206578

Ganti, A. (2022, January 9). *What Is an Asset Class?* Investopedia. https://www.investopedia.com/terms/a/assetclasses.asp

Garrod, C. (2018, February). *Why is Crypto so important and should I care?* https://www.conyers.com/publications/view/why-is-crypto-so-important-and-should-i-care/

Grauschopf, S. (2021, April 28). *CAPTCHAs: What They Are and How to Solve Them.* LiveAbout. https://www.liveabout.com/captchas-what-they-are-and-why-they-re-so-hard-to-enter-896946

Hardy, J. (2021, November 15). *The History of Bitcoin: A Complete Timeline of the Start of Web3.* https://historycooperative.org/?s=history+of+bitcoin

Holmes, F. (2021, December 20). *The Metaverse Is A $1 Trillion Revenue Opportunity. Here's How To Invest...* Forbes. https://www.forbes.com/sites/greatspeculations/2021/12/20/the-metaverse-is-a-1-trillion-revenue-opportunity-heres-how-to-invest/

Hougen, A. (2021, November 6). *The Facebook 2021 Rebrand: What Is Meta?* Cloudwards. https://www.cloudwards.net/facebook-rebrand/

Hum, T. (2022, January 19). *Metaverse barriers to entry are 'rather high:' CoinDesk Macro Editor.* https://www.msn.com/en-us/news/technology/metaverse-barriers-to-entry-are-e2-80-98rather-high-e2-80-99-coindesk-global-macro-editor/ar-AASWAGG

Hwang, I. (2021, February 16). *What is Fiat Currency? How is it Different from Crypto?* SoFi. https://www.sofi.com/learn/content/fiat-currency/

Iredale, G. (2021a, February 9). *Why Blockchain is Important in 2021 and Beyond—101 Blockchains.*

https://101blockchains.com/why-blockchain-is-important/

Iredale, G. (2021b, August 11). Top 10 Blockchain Adoption Challenges. *101 Blockchains*. https://101blockchains.com/blockchain-adoption-challenges/

Isberto, M. (2021, August 17). What Is Metaverse? *Colocation America*. https://www.colocationamerica.com/blog/metaverse-what-is-it

Java T Point. (2021). *Computer Network Architecture*. Www.Javatpoint.Com. https://www.javatpoint.com/computer-network-architecture

Kraken. (2022). *Ethereum vs Bitcoin*. https://www.kraken.com/en-us/compare/ethereum-vs-bitcoin

Lielacher, A. (2021, September 25). *Investing in the Metaverse: 4 Ways to Invest in Virtual Future*. https://cryptonews.com/exclusives/investing-in-the-metaverse-4-ways-to-invest-in-virtual-future.htm

Loiler, T. (2021, October 30). *The Metaverse: Challenges and Opportunities for Financial Services*. https://www.linkedin.com/pulse/metaverse-challenges-opportunities-financial-services-thibaut-loilier/

Luminos Mining. (2021). *10 Explanations On Why Crypto Currency Is Important.* https://luminosmining.com/10-explanations-on-why-crypto-currency-is-important/

Mayank. (2019, April 8). The Time is Now: Should You Invest in Crypto ASAP? *Tricky Enough.* https://www.trickyenough.com/should-you-invest-in-crypto/

McMillan, R. (2014, March 3). *The Inside Story of Mt. Gox, Bitcoin's $460 Million Disaster.* Wired. https://www.wired.com/2014/03/bitcoin-exchange/

Metaverse ICO Pad. (n.d.). *Why is the Metaverse important?* Retrieved January 10, 2022, from https://metaverseicopad.com/why-is-the-metaverse-important/

Milton, A. (2021, April 27). *What Is a Fungible Investment?* The Balance. https://www.thebalance.com/definition-of-the-trading-term-fungible-1031163

Mirakhmedov, A. (2021, October 22). *The Challenges of Industrial-Scale Bitcoin Mining.* https://www.nasdaq.com/articles/the-challenges-of-industrial-scale-bitcoin-mining-2021-10-22

Mitchell, C. (2021, September 1). *What Is a Sub-Asset Class?* Investopedia.

https://www.investopedia.com/terms/s/suba sset_class.asp

Motra, R. (2020, April 24). *What is Web 3.0? The Evolution of the Internet.* Blockgeeks. https://blockgeeks.com/guides/web-3-0/

Nakamoto, S. (n.d.). *Bitcoin: A Peer-to-Peer Electronic Cash System.* 9.

Newsfile Corp. (2021, November 25). *MetaFinance Rebuilds Financial Order of the Metaverse, Announces New Features At Its One-Year Halving Anniversary.* https://finance.yahoo.com/news/metafinanc e-rebuilds-financial-order-metaverse-082500725.html

Novak, M. (2021a, January 4). *TikTok Influencer Apologizes After Promoting Scam "Mando" Cryptocurrency.* Gizmodo. https://gizmodo.com/tiktok-influencer-apologizes-after-promoting-scam-mando-1846596562

Novak, M. (2021b, January 11). *Squid Game Cryptocurrency Scammers Make Off With $2.1 Million.* Gizmodo. https://gizmodo.com/squid-game-cryptocurrency-scammers-make-off-with-2-1-m-1847972824

Novak, M. (2021c, October 29). *New Squid Game Cryptocurrency Launches as Obvious Scam*. Gizmodo. https://gizmodo.com/new-squid-game-cryptocurrency-launches-as-obvious-scam-1847961584

Reahard, J. (2013, January 24). *Trion to publish ArcheAge in the West*. Massively by Joystiq. https://web.archive.org/web/20141220104552/http://massively.joystiq.com/2013/01/24/trion-to-publish-archeage-in-the-west/

Real Vision Finance. (2021, November 24). *The Metaverse Is the New Solar System*. https://www.youtube.com/watch?v=O1_LrREYQ8c

R.R.H. (2019, October 9). *Why is Blockchain Important More Than Ever?* Cryptomaniaks. https://cryptomaniaks.com/why-is-blockchain-important

Russel, S., & Norvig, P. (2020). *Artificial Intelligence: A modern approach* (4th ed.). Pearson.

Sahu, M. (2020, February 14). *Why Blockchain is Important? 21 Reasons That Shows How Blockchain Transforms the World*. https://www.upgrad.com/blog/why-blockchain-is-important/

Scott-Briggs, A. (2022, January 17). Banking and the Metaverse—The Future of Finance.

TechBullion. https://techbullion.com/banking-and-the-metaverse-the-future-of-finance/

Silver, C. (n.d.). *Council Post: What Is Web 3.0?* Forbes. Retrieved January 21, 2022, from https://www.forbes.com/sites/forbestechcouncil/2020/01/06/what-is-web-3-0/

Simplilearn. (2021, December 16). *What is Blockchain Technology and How Does It Work?* Simplilearn.Com. https://www.simplilearn.com/tutorials/blockchain-tutorial/blockchain-technology

Srinivas, R., & Sirsalewala, M. (2021, December 17). *Log4j Explained: How It Is Exploited and How to Fix It.* CISO MAG | Cyber Security Magazine. https://cisomag.eccouncil.org/log4j-explained/

Strange Loop Games. (n.d.). *Eco: Build A Civilization in a Simulated Ecosystem.* Retrieved January 25, 2022, from https://play.eco/

The Zimbabwean - Nation Online. (2021, August 9). *The Hyperinflation Hype: What really happened in Zimbabwe?* The Zimbabwean. https://www.thezimbabwean.co/2021/08/the-hyperinflation-hype-what-really-happened-in-zimbabwe/

Underwood, K. (2021, December 22). *How Many Websites Run on AWS? Outages Plague the Service.* Market Realist. https://marketrealist.com/p/how-many-websites-run-on-aws/

Vengupal, R. (2021, November 25). *What is Blockchain: Blockchain Definition, Features and Use Case.* Simplilearn.Com. https://www.simplilearn.com/tutorials/blockchain-tutorial/what-is-blockchain

Wallabit Media LLC. (2022). *How Many Bitcoins Are There?* https://www.buybitcoinworldwide.com/how-many-bitcoins-are-there/

Wang, P. (2021, November 3). *Why the Metaverse Matters.* https://www.gather.town/post/why-the-metaverse-matters

Yadron, D. (2016, June 8). We've seen Magic Leap's device of the future, and it looks like Merlin's skull cap. *The Guardian.* https://www.theguardian.com/technology/2016/jun/07/magic-leap-headset-design-patent-virtual-reality

Printed in Great Britain
by Amazon